Into the
Wild Blue
and Beyond

True stories of alien contact and military
aviation from the pages of The Star Beacon,
MUFON Journal and other publications,
plus guest stories from leading UFO researchers

James Parsons

Into the Wild Blue and Beyond

James Parsons

Earth Star Publications
Pagosa Springs, Colorado

First Printing July 2013

ISBN 978-0-944851-36-4

Cover artist: Ursula Freer, *"Here They Come"*

Published in the United States of America

Acknowledgments

First and foremost, I want to thank Ann Miller. Without her help and input, this book would not have been born. For more than 25 years Ann has carried the torch for UFOs and channeled information in the pages of *The Star Beacon*, a treasure trove of stories and reviews. Many thanks, Ann.

And to my wife, Bella, and to Dave Carson, and other friends in Taos, who accompanied me to conferences and shared their views on UFOs.

A few guest reviews and articles are included here also. My thanks to the writers and researchers who have furthered the Truth of UFOs and shared their stories at conferences and in print with me, and a public eager for information.

As it says in the Good Book, let those with ears to hear, hear, and those with eyes, see. There's a brave new world almost upon us, and the last thing we should do is fear it.

Contents

Sweden to investigate the Meier Case and further authenticate Meier's books and videos. Stevens' voice, like many others, is greatly missed.)

Introduction

After writing book reviews and articles for *The Star Beacon* and other publications for years, I decided to assemble a UFO book of reviews. Why? Because most folks don't read books these days and they miss some great stories about this field. While a few of these stories are on the Internet, most are not. Further, UFO books and stories reveal an important aspect of the hidden history of America, now coming into the light.

Research into the Roswell and Aztec cases prove that UFOs own our skies and are guided by aliens who come and go as they wish. Who are these visitors and why are they here? Are they friend or foe? What can we share with them and learn from them? The questions go on and on.

Some of the answers are found in the many books and reviews discussed and listed below. Now some important UFO history.

Unknown to the general public, in July 1947, President Truman directed General Nathan Twining to visit New Mexico shortly after the Roswell crash and report on what had happened there. Twining, a three-star general and head of Army Air Force Materiel Command, sends notice to Truman that the crash and bodies are "not of this Earth." For documentation of these events, see *The Day After Roswell*, 1997, Introduction and chapters four and five, the Majestic Documents, 1998, and MAJIC Eyes Only, 2004, by Wood and Wood Enterprises or Majesticdocuments.com.

In September 1947, Twining notifies the Intelligence Command that UFOs are "real and not visionary or fictitious." Although once secret, Twining's advisory to the Intelligence Command has been available to the public for decades through CAUS (Citizens Against UFO Secrecy) and Freedom of Information reports.

Twining becomes the "architect" of the UFO cover-up, according to Corso in *The Day After Roswell,* chapter five. A UFO working group is set up composed of 12 members—six military, six civilian. "Deny everything," Twining said to his superiors, "but allow public sentiment to take its course." Twining's statement becomes US government policy—secrecy, then gradual release of information about UFOs to the public.

In *The Day After Roswell*, Colonel Corso and his co-author Bill Birnes relate how and why the US Government decided to keep the whole subject a deep black secret. The rest of Corso's book tells his story of taking the artifacts recovered at Roswell, including night vision eye pieces, fiber optics, lasers, and integrated circuit chips, to US Defense contractors for exploitation. An amazing story, in this reviewer's opinion. At a UFO conference in Laughlin, Nevada, Corso's co-author Birnes told us Corso's revelations were part of the gradual release of information.

Another key figure in the story of UFOs is Harvard psychiatrist John Mack. Mack learned from researcher Budd Hopkins that abductions were real. Hopkins offered Mack some cases to explore through hypnosis. After exploring a number of cases, Mack wrote *Abduction*, 1994, and *Passport to the Cosmos*, 1999, detailing his own case histories, and analysis.

Mack became a high profile believer in UFOs. Mack spoke at least twice at conferences which I attended. His research got him into trouble at Harvard, Mack told us. A peer review group was convened; Mack was cleared of wrong doing, and Mack's attorney spoke with the president of Harvard. "He disturbed the Reality, that's why he got in trouble," the Harvard president said.

At a UFO conference in 2002 Mack said, "If people can't see it, it's because they refuse to see it. The experience is real."

Sadly, Mack lost his life in a hit and run accident in London in 2004. Then in 2011, Budd Hopkins passed. Their voices are greatly missed.

Enough of history. It's time to go into the wild blue and beyond.

Chapter 1

Evolution of a True Believer

"Don't bother me with the facts, my mind is made up."
—Stanton Friedman
having some fun with a debunker

One day in May 2011, a Taos man by the name of Andy Byrd phoned me. Byrd and his wife had recently seen a large green fireball pass over their house on Tune Drive, west of Taos.

"It was huge," Byrd said. "Green with a purple core." He told me it made no sound as it traveled east toward Taos Pueblo. He and his wife observed it for four or five seconds.

It looked like it was on a slant toward the ground, Byrd related. "My wife and I jumped in the car and tried to follow it, or locate the crash if it crashed."

They did not see it again, but they did locate a neighbor who saw it.

The great wave of green fireballs in the US happened in northern New Mexico in 1948-'49. (Obviously they still show up occasionally.) By chance I was a student at UNM during those years and enrolled in Astronomy

101 and 102. The fireballs were seen by both military and airline pilots approaching Albuquerque on the shared runways at Kirtland Air Force Base. The sightings were numerous and made the daily papers. They were described as round balls of green fire the size of basketballs and not unlike military flares or meteors. The fireballs were also observed over Sandia and Los Alamos National Laboratories.

On the last day of Astronomy 102 at UNM, we students were given an opportunity to ask our professor, Dr. Lincoln LaPaz, what they were. Dr. LaPaz was not only a full professor of Astronomy, but a nationally recognized expert on meteors.

Dr. LaPaz said the fireballs were not meteors because the characteristics weren't right. They were silent and changed direction. They flew slower than meteors and they apparently did not crash because LaPaz had been out searching for fragments without success.

"Then what are they?" we asked.

"I can tell you this," our professor said, "they are not natural."

More about these fireballs later.

In 1953 I graduated from UNM and entered the Air Force for navigation training. The training was like college, only the subjects were aeronautics, map reading, meteorology, electronics, radio, radar, and celestial. Training for me was followed by two years of extensive flying as crew navigator in transport aircraft over the Atlantic, Pacific and Alaskan theaters. On these flights I kept an eye out for green fireballs, but did not see any— nor did our pilots, so far as I know.

I did, however, discover the books by Major Donald Keyhoe—*Flying Saucers from Outer Space* (1954) and *Flying Saucer Conspiracy* (1955). I loved this one case which

Keyhoe reports on in *Conspiracy*. A B-29 was flying over the Gulf of Mexico. The crew spotted three flights of saucer-shaped craft in the air. The date was December 6, 1952.

The UFOs were sighted near dawn and appeared on the bomber's radar as well as visually, according to Keyhoe. The crew watched as a huge craft of unknown origin appeared and "swallowed" one of the flights. The giant UFO which Keyhoe called a "mother" ship then took off at 9,000 mph, according to the three radars on board the B-29.

When the bomber landed, its three radars were inspected and found to be in perfect condition. According to Keyhoe, the Air Force tried to suppress this story, but it was too late. Keyhoe had reported on the sighting and released it. Major Keyhoe, a former Marine pilot, was a great UFO researcher and all ufologists owe him a debt of gratitude as well as for tips on how to be a successful ufologist.

On the final pages of my well-worn copy of *Flying Saucers from Outer Space,* Keyhoe shares the official letter he received from the Air Force, saying that if the maneuvers reported are correct, then the saucers are from space. In Appendix II of his book, Keyhoe lists 51 military UFO sightings obtained legally from the Air Force, hard evidence for saucer reality.

By the time I left the Air Force, I knew UFOs were spacecraft and probably from another planet. How did I know? Because of extreme angle turns, the speeds they attained, and because of the books and sightings reported by Keyhoe.

Nathan Twining

As time passed I learned other key aspects of the flying saucer mystery. One of the outstanding men in the history of the Air Force was a three-star general by the name of Nathan Twining.

Twining, in charge of Air Materiel Command and scientific labs, flew to New Mexico on July 7, 1947, for four days during the time period of the Roswell crash and recovery. Researcher Stanton Friedman was able to prove the general's travel plan by uncovering Twining's and his pilot's flight logs (*Crash at Corona*).

According to *The Day After Roswell,* Twining reported to President Truman upon his return from Roswell, shared craft recovery details with the president and informed him that the occupants were "not of this world."

On Sept. 23, 1947, Twining issued a secret advisory to Air Force Intelligence, saying that flying saucers are "something real and not visionary or fictitious." Twining's memo described the saucers as "disc-shaped" and the size of "man-made aircraft," with extraordinary flying characteristics, according to *Crash at Corona* and *The Roswell Incident.*

A key player in the unfolding story of Roswell and UFOs, Twining became Air Force Chief of Staff (when I served in the '50s) and Chairman of the Joint Chiefs. If Twining said, "UFOs are real," then they are, or so I believed then and now. Another true believer is Nathan Twining, Jr., the general's son, a strong advocate for the reality of the saucers. Twining, Jr., lives in Albuquerque and has been interviewed several times by researchers. A friend of this writer asked Twining, Jr., why he was so sure flying saucers were real. "My father told me," he replied.

UFOs in Space

Fast forward to the 1970s. I had moved to Santa Fe, New Mexico, and was in the midst of a fast and furious career as an art dealer. I didn't have time for UFOs, or so I thought. I did, however, join a discussion and a metaphysical group headed by a woman named Theodora Anderson. At her meetings we often discussed UFOs and occasionally watched videos on this subject. We were also regular visitors to a Santa Fe nonprofit by the name of The Space Science Center.

At the Center the public and school classes could view videos on the Training of Astronauts, The Bermuda Triangle, and UFOs. One day the Center's genial owner, C. de Baca, said to me, "I wrote NASA for anything they had on UFOs. Would you like to see what they sent?" *Would I?*

Soon we were sitting inside the darkened theater, the projector running. On the screen I saw an astronaut aboard a space ship, holding up a sign which said, "Apollo 8 home movies." Behind him, another astronaut held a camera aimed out a porthole at two objects in space. The two objects appeared to be following alongside Apollo 8. They were oval in shape but hazy, not clearly defined. The film continued for a few minutes, then ended abruptly.

I stopped by the Space Science Center the next day, to ask de Baca if he would make me a copy of the film. "You're too late," de Baca said. "The FBI from Santa Fe called on me and asked for the film. They said NASA wanted it back and they took it."

Someone at NASA tried to do us a favor, I recall thinking. This is another example of the alleged government UFO coverup, which all ufologists know about.

When *Above Top Secret* by Timothy Good was published in 1988, there were several pages describing what the astronauts saw in space. Good quoted Maurice Chatelain, chief designer of Apollo communications, as saying in his autobiography that all Apollo and Gemini flights "were followed ... by space vehicles of extra-terrestrial origin—flying saucers or UFOs ... if you want to call them that."

Chatelain wrote that Mission Control then ordered "absolute silence" about what the astronauts had seen.

When Good contacted Neil Armstrong about what they had seen in space, Armstrong said, "All Apollo observations on all Apollo flights were reported to the public." The facts remain controversial among ufologists.

Chatelain, in his autobiography, went on to state that "Santa Claus" was a code word used around NASA for flying saucers. When James Lovell rounded the moon in the Apollo 8 command module, the first words he said were, "Please be informed that there is a Santa Claus." It was Christmas Day 1968. Could Lovell have had a hidden meaning in those words? Could the Apollo 8 film, which I viewed long ago, have shown alien spacecraft, as I believe?

A few months passed. I had not had a real vacation in years. It was time for a walkabout and our discussion leader, Theodora, had an idea. She wanted me to contact a California group calling itself "The Majic Cirkus," and travel with them. Soon, with two friends, I headed to a place called Giant Rock in the California desert. But before we practiced the dances with the theater group, we stopped by the home of George Van Tassel, a known flying saucer contactee living near the Giant Rock airport.

We were welcomed at Van Tassel's home, but he was at Sunday lunch with his family in another room. After he finished, he came to where we were sitting, and we began a conversation.

Rather quickly he sized us up as well-meaning folks, but without real knowledge of UFOs. He therefore began a history of this subject for our education. He told us of

Kenneth Arnold's now famous sighting of the nine "flying discs" over Mount Rainier in Washington state in June 1947. This he followed with a retelling of his own close encounter with an extraterrestrial being.

While sleeping outdoors in his sleeping bag at Giant Rock, he heard footsteps. A being approached Van Tassel and asked him if he wanted to help his people. According to Van Tassel, he was led to a space ship which had "landed" above ground nearby. Later, the being channeled information to Van Tassel on how to build a machine. Van Tassel, an aeronautical engineer, had begun work on the machine which was housed in a structure nearby.

"Is the machine to be a source of free energy?" we asked.

"No, it is to be a time machine to rejuvenate minds and bodies as people pass within its force field."

Then Van Tassel talked about Roswell and said the case was a true crash of a UFO. A saucer had been recovered by the military, Van Tassel said, near Roswell, and covered up on orders from higher headquarters. He talked about a second crash a year later in New Mexico, and how it also had been covered up. We could read the story of the second crash by Frank Scully in *Behind the Flying Saucers*, Van Tassel said.

This was an ear-popping conversation for me because in those days (1977) almost no one spoke of UFO crashes as true events. Many folks still don't believe. I couldn't wait to share this information with our group in Santa Fe, and to read Scully's book.

When I returned to Santa Fe, I did share the information with our discussion group. As I reported on the story, Theodora, seated across the room, jumped up and said, "I know about this. Let me tell you what I know."

She then launched into her story, which we had not

heard before. She and her husband, Thurston, a pilot, were friends with a colonel at Kirtland Air Force Base. The colonel was in charge of security at the base. The colonel told Theo and her husband that Roswell was a true event, which had been covered up and remained a closely guarded secret. The colonel also related how bodies were recovered, one remaining alive. Our good friends, Theo and Thurston, now deceased, were full of surprises.

Here in the space of two short weeks was a second report that Roswell was a true crash. Interesting! The next year, 1978, Stanton Friedman, the premier UFO researcher, in my opinion, met face to face with Major Jesse Marcel, the former base intelligence officer at Roswell Army Air Field in 1947. Marcel told Friedman that the materials he (Marcel) recovered at Roswell were most likely from somewhere else, not Earth, and were not the materials which General Ramey exhibited before the press a few days after the crash. Marcel's statements are vital to the unfolding story of Roswell and later were recorded on video.

This meeting with Marcel caused Friedman to begin research on the Roswell case in earnest, resulting in the publication, with William Moore, ufologist, and Charles Berlitz, writer, of *The Roswell Incident* (1980). I inhaled that paperback, a third report that crashes were real. Friedman is known as a careful scientist/researcher who digs for facts and leaves the speculation to others.

With the publication of *The Roswell Incident* (1980), it was as if a dam broke. Other pro-Roswell accounts followed: *The Encyclopedia of UFOs* (1980); *Clear Intent* (1984); *Crash at Aztec* (1986); *Above Top Secret* (1988); *Crash at Corona* (1992); *Conspiracy of Silence* (1997); *The Day After Roswell* (1997); *The UFO Book* (1998);

UFOs and the National Security State (2000); *Witness to Roswell* (2007); *Flying Saucers and Science* (2008); *The Roswell Legacy* (2008), to mention just a few pro-UFO accounts.

An Unforgettable Sighting

In September 1978, I went with an Edgar Cayce research group to Bimini in the Bahamas. Cayce is widely known in metaphysical circles as America's foremost psychic, now deceased since 1945. Cayce said that Atlantis was a real civilization with the remains now covered up by the Atlantic Ocean. We were on our way to dive on the "Stones of Atlantis." *Fabulous eight-day trip* ... but the story I want to relate here happened on the return to Miami at night.

I was at the helm of our vessel, a 38 ft. sloop, on the 10 p.m. to 2 a.m. shift. A lady named Dottie Lange was assigned as our "go-fer," to go for coffee and the captain below decks, if he were needed.

Around midnight, I had just finished telling Dottie of the Fate of Flight 19, a mysterious aircraft disappearance at sea in Bahama waters.

Dottie said to me, "Jim, there are two blue lights following our craft. Would you turn around and tell me what they are?" Dottie sat in front of me and could see clearly aft. I crammed my head around and saw two blue lights. "They look like lights on a ship or a ship's mast," I said.

Then I heard Dottie exclaim, "Here they come."

The two lights pulled up right beside our open cockpit vessel, only they were huge, one the size of a two-story house, the other two-thirds that size, vibrating blue and white radiations in perfect oval patterns. *Awesome.*

"Get the captain," I told Dottie. "He won't believe his eyes."

One of the two shapes threw a bright light over our vessel, like a searchlight. *These objects are no swarm of bees and no mirage either*, I recall thinking.

As our captain came through the hatch doorway, silently, swiftly the lights pulled back. Captain Foster saw only two blue lights in the distance as I had originally seen.

Dottie: "What in God's name was that?"

Me: "Have you ever seen a UFO?"

Dottie: "No."

Me: "Well, now you have. Two of them."

A few minutes later, smiling, I said to Dottie, "We are passing through the Bermuda Triangle. What did you expect?"

There was a second vessel traveling behind us on this Atlantis research trip. When we docked at Miami, the watch on that other larger vessel reported they saw nothing. However, their helm and steering was below decks, unlike the open cockpit steering set-up of our vessel. Their visibility was more restricted. Or perhaps the sighting was for Dottie and I only?

My study of ufology has been a great awakening as well as a learning experience. Shortly before Bella and I were married in 1988, I learned that my wife had a sighting of a UFO out her bedroom window as a 10-year-old. She is a true believer, as much as I am. Together we go to conferences, talk to folks about their experiences, visit crash sites, read the books, and have a real good time.

Now back to those green fireballs. Soon after the great Wave of 1948-'49, a two-day conference was held at Los Alamos to determine what exactly was on their doorstep. Scientists who had seen the fireballs, including Dr. LaPaz, were present.

According to Dolan in *UFOs and the National*

Security State, the majority of scientists believed the fireballs were meteors, or a new type of meteor. An ET (extraterrestrial) explanation was "studiously avoided." Such an explanation was "off limits," according to Dolan. So much for the open minds of scientists, except for LaPaz, who told the scientists the objects were "surely artificial."

Clark in *The UFO Book* discussed at length several government and army reports in which green fireballs appeared not only over New Mexico nuclear facilities, but during the same years (1948-'49) over a nuclear storage facility at Killen, Texas, inside Fort Hood. The fireballs, usually intense green or yellow-green, were in some cases tiny, only inches in diameter and observed a few feet above the ground.

From this writer's recent study of fireballs, it would appear that balls of fire are of two distinct types: *Conventional meteors*, which burn up in Earth's atmosphere, and are seen as white light streaks in the night sky, and *green balls,* which are not meteors at all. These green fireballs have an intense color, make no sound, exhibit no cosmic dust trail, fly slower than meteors at lower altitudes, and are capable of changing direction or maintaining level flight. Apparently they have never crashed.

My best guess is they are probes from UFOs in deep space, on surveillance missions.

Crashed Saucers

One of the UFO conferences which I attended on a regular basis over the past 15 years is the International UFO Congress and Film Festival, which was held at Laughlin, Nevada. There one could meet and talk with researchers, abductees and kindred spirits from all over the planet.

I became acquainted with Wendelle Stevens, the UFO researcher from Tucson, retired Air Force fighter pilot and founder of the Congress. Stevens shared with many of us a case he had researched concerning crashed saucers. Here's the case:

A guard from Area 51, the top secret Nevada base, had deserted and contacted Stevens. The guard told Stevens he was a member of the Delta Force and that one of his jobs was guarding crashed saucers at the underground facility #S4. This is a complicated case and I am going to abbreviate it here.

The guard drew pictures for Stevens of the saucers housed at Area 51 in underground bays. These were shown on the big screen at the conference. Stevens, narrating, said he sat on this information for 10 years until he could confirm it. Confirmation arrived when another military man, a colonel, contracted a fatal disease at Area 51 and was allowed to go to Italy to die. UFO researchers from that country interviewed the colonel in the hospital.

At the request of researchers, the colonel painted a picture of a crashed saucer in one of the bays at Area 51. Stevens received photos of the painting, the subject of which was very similar to the drawings from 10 years before. *Bingo.* Stevens decided to reveal what he had learned. The complete story with photos of drawings is available through the International UFO Congress and Film Festival, *www.ufocongress.com* (2001).

One might question the motives of researchers like Stevens in revealing facts which may involve classified information, but in my opinion the people have a right to know that saucers are real, have crashed, and that we are being visited. In most cases, divulging this information doesn't hurt anybody or get them killed. The Supreme

Court has protected whistleblowers where the public interest was great.

Stevens died in 2010. I will long cherish the two breakfasts I shared with him and his generosity in sharing information with myself and the conference.

In my opinion, Keyhoe, Stevens and Friedman are national heroes.

One more Roswell/Albuquerque story and then I'll close. In July 1947, Albuquerque newsman Frank Joyce worked for KGFL in Roswell. Mac Brazel, the rancher who brought crash debris into Roswell and showed it to Sheriff Wilcox, was put on the phone with Joyce.

Brazel told Joyce that he had not only observed what is now called "the debris field," but bodies as well. This part of the Roswell story Joyce did not share with researchers until after he retired from his news job with KOB in Albuquerque.

In May 1998, researchers Carey and Schmitt interviewed Joyce, the third or fourth interview for Schmitt. Joyce said, "Boys, I am going to tell you something I have never shared before."

According to Joyce, when he was on the phone with Brazel in July 1947, Brazel was very upset. Brazel described bodies decaying in the desert. "Oh, the stench," Brazel said. "The stench. What am I going to do?"

"What stench? What are you talking about?" Joyce said.

"Little people," Brazel said. "Unfortunate little creatures."

The full, fascinating story, along with the revised Walter Haut* story, is related in *Witness to Roswell* (2007).

Piece by piece, the Roswell Incident continues to unfold. The public should keep an open mind about green fireballs and those mysterious UFOs.

* Walter Haut is the co-founder of the Roswell UFO Museum and an eyewitness to a crashed saucer.

Chapter 2

Crash Landing at Aztec

The following chapter is based on *Behind the Flying Saucers*, Scully (1950); *Crash at Aztec, A Well Kept Secret*, Steinman and Stevens (1986); a lecture by Linda Moulton Howe, Aztec Symposium (2005), and six trips to the symposium by the reviewer.

The crash-landing of a UFO at Aztec is one of the great stories of 20th century USA. Read on, and see if you agree.

Columnist Frank Scully was the first writer to alert and inform the public that a disabled flying saucer had landed on a mesa 12 miles northeast of Aztec, New Mexico. Aztec is a small northern New Mexico town near Farmington.

In his best-selling book *Behind the Flying Saucers* (1950), Scully claimed that a saucer had landed and was observed by locals and oil workers on the morning of March 25, 1948. (Aztec was an oil town, like Farmington.) The craft appeared to be intact except for a fracture in one porthole, according to Scully. It was silver in color, circular, and almost 100 ft. in diameter

with a dome on top.

The cabin feature measured 18 ft. in diameter. The craft lay on the mesa, tilted, due to the hump on the bottom. Sixteen bodies—all dead—were inside. (Bodies later revised to 14.)

This was a sensational story and one which many sophisticated folks, who were not there, would find impossible to believe.

Frank Scully

A couple who were at the crash site and lived nearby told locals to stay off the unknown craft, according to Scully. Locals were also told the military had been notified. Later the couple was taken to their nearby home and sworn to secrecy.

Military and Scientific Teams arrive

Within a short time a helicopter was heard flying overhead. A security team arrived and took charge. Onlookers were divided into groups, sworn to secrecy, names taken and folks ordered away from the area.

Hours later, a team of scientists arrived. They had flown into Durango, Colorado, and had been shuttled to the site, probably by auto. After marveling at the uniqueness of the circular craft, they set about gaining entry. Using a pole, they gained entry by widening a cracked porthole, pushing a button or lever, and a door opened on the side of the craft, according to Scully. Most of this is narration, hearsay and undocumented—and sounds like science fiction, doesn't it?

Scully reported that he obtained his information from Silas Newton, an oil man and investor, and from a mysterious "Dr. Gee." He further explained that Dr. Gee was really a composite of eight scientists who were at the crash site, some of whom Scully talked with. Dr. Gee was revealed to be an Arizona magnetics engineer who was an associate of one of the eight scientists, but the other names were never revealed.

In a strange turn of events, Scully's story was sought after by a San Francisco journalist by the name of Cahn, who wanted to buy Scully's story. Scully refused to sell and Cahn turned jealous and vowed to "get" Scully.

Cahn reported Scully to the FBI and other government agencies. He wrote an article for *True Magazine* and labeled Scully's story a hoax.

Cahn also prevailed upon the Denver D.A. to charge Scully with a crime-fraud. A trial ensued in which Newton and "Dr. Gee" (Lee GeBauer) were convicted by a jury. They paid court costs and received no other penalty.

The Federal Government declared the whole case a hoax. The case died, just like Roswell died after the Army said the crash at Roswell was a weather balloon. The public, including many UFO researchers, accepted the verdict. It was a hoax, people thought; case closed.

For the record, Newton, GeBauer and Scully maintained for the rest of their lives that they had learned the truth about UFOs and shared it with a public who deserved to know.

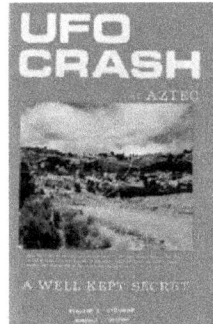

UFO Crash at Aztec, A Well Kept Secret

In 1981, an aerospace engineer by the name of William Steinman decided to take a look at the Aztec case. Steinman described himself as a skeptic, but he had read Scully's book and it raised questions in his mind. Did anything really happen in that small town?

Steinman went to Aztec, New Mexico, and began by

interviewing locals who knew about the story. At a yard sale he learned where the crash site was. He went there and observed charred rocks and a heavy concrete slab and he noted the remoteness of the site.

He listened and asked questions as locals replayed the story for him.

A UFO had landed or crash-landed at Hart Canyon, was recovered by the military and taken away. The craft was circular, silver in color, 100 ft. in diameter, with a dome on top and bottom. One porthole was fractured. Over a period of three days, the craft was dismantled and hauled at night by large flatbed trucks under tarps to a secure location thought to be Los Alamos. The area was secured by troops for two miles in each direction.

Steinman also reported that the craft had been detected by three radars operating in the Four Corners area. One of these was of a new type and more powerful than the others. One or more of these radars may have interfered with the ship's flight mechanism and caused it to pancake down to the mesa, according to Steinman.

The radar stations notified higher headquarters. A special Army unit, the Interplanetary Phenomenon Unit (don't you love that name?), operating out of Camp Hale, Colorado, was ordered to the scene. A team of scientists was also assembled and sent to the crash site. The scientists included two of the country's foremost men of science, Dr. Robert Oppenheimer and Dr. Vannevar Bush, according to Steinman.

There is some documentation in Steinman's book for some of these statements. Here is a telex sent from Camp Hale, Colo., to headquarters, Assistant Chief of Staff, G-2 (Army Intelligence), Washington, D.C., at the time of the recovery mission and reproduced on page 45 of Steinman's

Diameter: 99.9 feet overall   Height: 6.0 feet overall
Cabin: 18.0 feet across   Cabin to rim edge: 41.0 feet
Top of cabin: Raised 45" above the level of the mean plane of the disc
Disc edge: 27" above the saucer base, slightly curved slope upper and lower surface of disc

Line Drawing of the 100' diameter disc-shaped craft which came down at Azted, New Mexico on 25 March 1948. This reconstruction is from several eyewitness descriptions. Note the thin diameter to thickness ratio.

---

book:
"FLYING OBJECT OF UNKNOWN ORIGIN RECOVERED NEAR AZTEC, NM. CRAFT APPROX. 100 FEET DIAMETER, 30 FEET HEIGHT, ONE WINDOW, PORT BLOWN, BODIES ON BOARD. ALL OCCUPANTS DEAD, 4 FT. HEIGHT, OVERSIZED HEADS, CRAFT HAS METALIC SKÍN THIN AS NEWSPAPER, BUT TWO TOUGH TO PENETRATE BY CONVENTIONAL TOOLS, PRIVATE PROPERTY WAS PURCHASED FROM LOCALS IN ORDER TO FACILITATE TRANSPORTING OF THE CRAFT TO BASE."

There are other documents, exhibits and drawings scattered throughout the Steinman research text relating to more crashed saucers, MJ12 members, medical reports of bodies, Freedom of Information requests, security considerations. On the whole, good documentation but often hard to read, assimilate, and connect up with the text. This is a research book, not a relaxed read.

The scientist who leaked the whole Aztec crash story to "Dr. Gee" (Lee GeBauer), according to Steinman and Wendelle Stevens (publishers of the book), is named in and pictured in *Crash at Aztec*. Stevens had also been researching the case.

As most students of ufology know, the whole UFO

field is complicated and infused with disinformation and secrecy. Much of the story is classified top secret or above and remains classified to this day.

Steinman wrote to another scientist, Dr. Robert I. Sarbacher, who served on various boards and committees with Dr. Bush and other scientists who were believed to have been at the crash site and participated in the recovery. Steinman sought information from Sarbacher by letter and phone about the crash of 1948, 33 years later. Eventually, Sarbacher responded.

The crash was real, he told Steinman, and Drs. Bush, Oppenheimer and John Van Neuman, the country's most famous mathematician and computer designer, were present, he wrote.

Steinman writes that he was thrilled to receive Sarbacher's letter. It was confirmation of years of research. The letter is reproduced on pages 324-325 of the text.

Eventually Steinman ran out of time and money. He contacted Wendelle Stevens, veteran UFO researcher (now deceased), who agreed to publish Steinman's research along with his own. This resulted in their privately published book, *UFO Crash at Aztec, A Well Kept Secret* (1986).

It is well worth a read and study, but I'll save you the trouble. In the book, the Aztec story is related as true, although covered up by the government.

Steinman ended his first research trip to Aztec by reporting on the large black helicopters that followed him as he pursued his research, and flew over his home in California when he returned there.

Linda Moulton Howe
Presentation at Aztec

In March 2005, Linda Moulton Howe, longtime UFO

researcher, was a speaker at the Aztec conference. For years a story had circulated among UFO buffs like myself that there had been a huge flyover of UFOs over Farmington in 1950, two years after the alleged crash at Aztec of 1948.

Howe produced the front page of the *Farmington Daily Times* for March 18, 1950. She held the newspaper up. The banner headline screamed at the small gathering of the public and researchers, my wife and I included.

Linda Moulton Howe

HUGE SAUCER ARMADA
JOLTS FARMINGTON

In the story that followed, scores of people in Farmington described the objects in the skies as "silvery disks," many flying in formation. One observer, Brooks—a former WWII tail gunner—said the objects could not be aircraft because of the way they maneuvered, made right-angle turns, and stood on their edges. Howe produced other creditable witnesses who verified these observations, either on tape or in person.

Howe brought a man named Eaton to the conference from Pennsylvania. Eaton, age 29 at the time of the great Aztec/Farmington flyover, was shocked at what he saw in the skies overhead—silvery discs, perhaps 100 or more, one a red/orange color, moving fast back and forth over Farmington. Eaton had been in the Navy Air Corps and knew his aircraft, he commented. Eaton also spoke of the large cigar-shaped craft he had seen over Farmington traveling with five smaller UFOs. Sounds like a memorial flyover to me, I recall thinking, like a flyover I participated in during my Air Force days.

Military officers showed up in Farmington, Eaton said; they told witnesses, "They are military experimental aircraft—forget about them." "No, they aren't," Eaton answered. One military guy said they may be balloons. Eaton said, "I don't drink and they aren't balloons."

Howe attacked the government policy of silence and denial about UFOs in her talk. Knowledge gives us strength, she said. "We are not alone."

Author of at least four books and her documentary "Alien Harvest," Howe's Web site is at *EarthFiles.com*.

The Aztec Incident

The Aztec Incident: Recovery at Hart Canyon (2011) by Scott and Suzanne Ramsey and associates with a foreword by Stanton Friedman and a preface by William Steinman

Review by James Parsons

Introduction

When Suzanne Ramsey was about 7 years old, she recalls her mom reading *Behind the Flying Saucers* by Frank Scully. She also recalls her parents thinking about a move to a warmer climate.

In her introduction to *The Aztec Incident,* Suzanne recalled how her parents decided on a move to Aztec, New Mexico, where the flying saucer crash they had read about allegedly happened. In time, the family moved to Aztec.

34

Years later as a grownup, Suzanne hosted an interview radio program. She interviewed Scott Ramsey about his passion (UFOs) and the rest, as they say, is history—mutual respect, admiration, friendship, marriage, shared UFO research, shared values and UFO travels.

In Chapter One Scott Ramsey interviews an oil worker by the name of Doug Noland, who claimed he and his boss, Bill Ferguson, were directed to the crash landing site on the early morning of March 25, 1948, because of a burning fire near company oil tanks in that area. On that morning Noland and Ferguson got the surprise of their lives. They observed a craft of unknown origin sitting on a mesa with a few other oil workers viewing the craft.

In 2003, Noland told Ramsey that he and his boss (Ferguson) saw a huge circular craft, silver/aluminum in color, with a bubble on top resting on the mesa. Other oil workers were present as well as a few locals. Some climbed on top of the craft.

A police officer was at the site, Noland said. The officer told Noland he had followed the strange circular craft from Cuba, New Mexico, to the mesa. The officer said the craft was flying slowly and "fluttered like a leaf" just prior to landing. Ramsey eventually identified the officer as Manuel Sandoval of the Town of Cuba.

Ramsey indicated Noland was a mature guy, respected by his peers. He had told his story a number of times to selected people, but now he wanted it on the record.

Noland related that both he and Ferguson climbed on the strange craft; they noted portholes, one with a hole in it. Peering inside, they could see two bodies slumped over what appeared to be a control panel.

Noland provided other details. The craft was smooth —perhaps 100 feet across—dome on top and another on the bottom; there were three gold rings around the outer edge, Noland said.

Noland said that his boss, Ferguson, used a fire pole off one of the oil trucks, poked through the hole in a porthole, touched a button or lever, and a door and stairs opened on the side of the craft.

Other oil workers said there were more bodies inside, charred a dark brown, and a helicopter was observed flying overhead. The bodies were small, like a child, someone said.

Soon the military showed up, divided the onlookers into groups and told folks it was a national security matter and they were not to discuss it with anyone.

Scott Ramsey, who has been researching the Aztec case for 25 years,

Doug Noland right with world renowned pilot John Lear, 1995
Courtesy Mike Price collection

located another eyewitness and interviewed him in 1999. Ken Farley told Ramsey that he and a friend were driving from the small town of Cidar Hill near Aztec. They heard of the commotion on Hart Canyon Road. They decided to have a look.

They observed a huge object lying on the ground with people around it. From their clothing, Farley said, most of the people appeared to be oil workers.

An older couple was also present, as Farley recalled. The couple warned folks to stay off the craft. No one paid attention to them. Later Ramsey learned the couple lived close to the crash site and their name was Knight. Like the other witnesses, they later said they had been sworn to secrecy.

Ken Farley's description of the craft was similar to the others the Ramseys had heard and read about— circular, huge, a dome on top, lying on the mesa at an angle of 12 degrees due to another hump on the bottom.

Another eyewitness was a minister from a small church in nearby Mancos, Colo. The minister, Solon Brown, had stopped at the crash landing site to see if he could be of help. Later that day, the minister told his deacon and a few board members in confidence what he had witnessed—a large craft and dead bodies. The deacon's son, grown up, told Ramsey the incredible story which he recalled clearly, although it had been many years since that day in 1948.

Behind the Flying Saucers

Chapter Two of the Ramseys' book is titled *Behind the Flying Saucers*. It reviews Frank Scully's book of that title discussed earlier in this chapter and told how the military had recovered a flying saucer "virtually intact."

Scully learned this story from the mysterious "Dr. Gee" (mentioned earlier, on page 28) and Silas Newton, an oil man and investor.

On a trip through the Southwest, Dr. Gee explained to Scully and Newton how the government had "tenescope observers" at Alamogordo and Los Alamos and other locations in New Mexico. The Aztec craft was observed, according to Dr. Gee. Military teams were alerted and sent to the crash landing site.

Dr. Gee, being a magnetics engineer and former government scientist, also explained to Scully and Newton about the several recovered flying saucers he had been privileged to observe in government laboratories, and about the Aztec craft, its dismantling and transport to a secure laboratory, believed to be Los Alamos. (Dr. Gee was identified as Lee Gebauer of Phoenix on another occasion by Scully and was also described as a composite of eight scientists who were at the Aztec crash site whose names have never been revealed.)

The craft was powered by magnetism, Dr. Gee explained, and the craft itself was a giant capacitor. The outer skin of the craft was aluminum, but of a kind unknown on Earth, according to Dr. Gee.

Bella Martin at the Aztec UFO crash site

In the chapter "Did Cahn Con the Cons," Ramsey wrote that writer Cahn vowed to "get" Scully when Scully refused to sell him Scully's story. Cahn initiated a criminal suit against Scully in Denver. He asked the

FBI to investigate Scully. He wrote an article in *True Magazine* calling Scully's story a hoax.

The government also called the Aztec story a hoax and the story died just as Roswell died when the military labeled it a weather balloon, eight months previously. But of course, Aztec wasn't dead and—like Roswell—only waiting to be investigated.

The Man Who Knew Too Much

Another key player in the unfolding story of Aztec is an oil man named Silas Newton. Newton was not only a geophysicist but a student of magnetic propulsion, according to Ramsey. It was Newton who first told Scully the Aztec story.

While researching the Frank Scully archives at the University of Wyoming, the Ramseys discovered an unpublished autobiography by Newton in Scully's archive. Ramsey writes that Newton was not only rich but well educated, literate, a man who understood that magnetic lines of force could propel a spaceship.

The Ramseys describe the amazing talk which Newton delivered at the University of Denver on March 8, 1950. In this lecture, Newton not only told a packed audience that flying saucers exist; he said they were propelled by magnetics using the sun and Earth's gravitational fields. One of these drawings is reproduced in the Ramsey book with notes by Newton. According to Ramsey, Newton devoted many pages of his autobiography to the science of magnetism and UFOs.

Ramsey describes the "Kafkaesque" trial which Newton was forced to undergo and convicted at in Denver. Newton described the attacks on him as a "nightmare," but he survived the trial with the only legal penalty the payment of court costs, $18,000. The jury said he was guilty of fraud with an investor's funds. Apparently no mention of flying saucers was allowed at the trial. Ramsey obtained his information about the trial from court documents but also from researcher James Moseley, who was present at the trial.

For the record, Newton, Scully and Dr. Gee maintained for the rest of their lives that the stories they told and wrote about were true; their only crime— speaking about a subject, parts of which are Top Secret and remain so to this day.

The primary difference between *The Aztec Incident* and the other two books about the case are that the Ramsey book is well organized and documented. The Ramsey book also includes numerous details not covered in this review such as finding the "lost" radar stations, the dismantling and transport of the craft over the probable route existing in 1948 and the replanting of the crash landing site after the recovery and burial of K rations and military artifacts found at the scene.

Through their study of the Aztec case, the Ramseys conclude that Scully and Newton were courageous and honorable men who attempted to reveal the truth about UFOs when doing so was taboo.

The book should take its place beside others by Dolan, Stevens, Friedman, Scully, Steinman, and all the other dedicated researchers who have labored to bring this and other UFO realities to the public awareness and into the light of day.

Well done, guys.

Chapter 3

Soulic Journeys
and the Great Shift

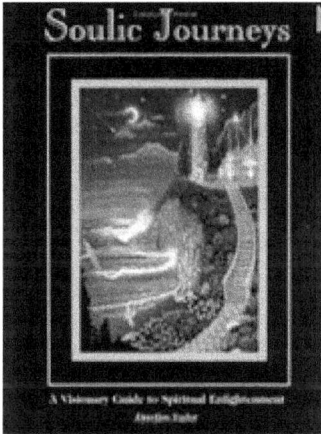

Soulic Journeys, a Visionary Guide to Spiritual Enlightenment
by Douglas Taylor
ISBN 978-0970459305

Douglas Taylor in *Soulic Journeys* takes his readers on a visionary UFO journey in both words and fine art. Much of the text is a result of a face-to-face encounter Taylor had inside a space craft with a starship commander and crew.

Artist Taylor describes himself as a surfer who, for more than 10 years, traveled the world seeking the perfect wave. The UFO field and fine arts were far from his field of interest during those years.

One day in 1978, tired from a day of surfing the sparkling Caribbean, he lay down on his bed in Puerto Rico. Before falling asleep, he experienced a "spinning sensation." His whole body began gyrating in various patterns. After a short time, he found himself standing inside what could only be described as a space craft.

"Yes Friend, you are truly with us," a being in a white suit said to him, while six other beings stood nearby in front of a control panel. The being in the white suit stared intently at Taylor as he spoke in the room, which was brilliantly lighted. *He is no human being,* Taylor thought, and he assumed he was on a ship from another planet. The being addressed Taylor using telepathy.

"You are one of many we are contacting to prepare you for the future," the being continued. Then he proceeded to tell Taylor things he should know, such as that their ship was cylindrical in shape, that they were from another solar system, that the universe was teeming with life, that our planet would experience great earth changes, and that their ship was powered by light radiation.

He pointed to a vertical tube that was in the room and explained its use in propulsion of their vehicle. There is more about the propulsion system, but it is quite technical.

Not long after this experience, Taylor awoke with a strong desire to learn to paint. Taylor's paintings and Giclée prints are fine art portraits of nature—oceans, dolphins, whales and, of course, of illuminated visions of cosmic space. Since his experience, Taylor has been offered numerous radio and TV interviews.

His book includes channeled essays on angels, guides and ascended masters, from years of study of metaphysics.

By coincidence, this reviewer was also in the Bermuda Triangle in 1978, not far from where Taylor had his experience. He was steering a 30 ft. sloop on an Edgar Cayce research trip. Around midnight, two glorious egg-shaped UFOs drew alongside our vessel, perhaps drawn by our conversation, which was a discussion of UFOs and the fate of Flight 19, a mysterious disappearance at sea.

I directed my associate, Dottie Lange, below decks to rouse the captain. The radiant ovoids switched off the light they had turned on and flew silently, swiftly across the waters. Captain Foster saw only two blue and white distant lights several miles away.

After this experience of UFOs, I became a writer of UFO subjects and began to attend conferences. I met Taylor at one of these conferences and bought his book. In my opinion, Taylor's experience is genuine and a unique view inside a starship along with a fascinating conversation.

Chapter 4

An Invitation to the Dance

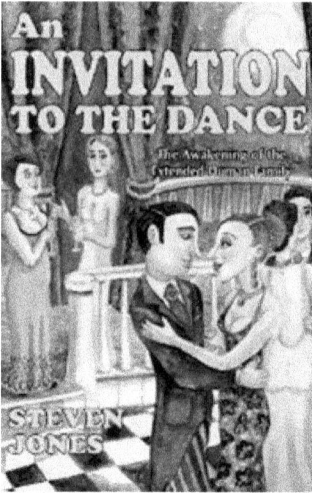

*An Invitation to the Dance,
The Awakening of the
Extended Human Family
by Stephen Jones, © 2010,
Little Star Publishing Co.
Essex, UK*

In his introduction to *An Invitation to the Dance*, Jones states he intends to tell us who the ETs really are and what their purpose is in contact at this time. Further, he plans to take us on a journey which may rattle our belief systems as it did for him.

Okay, I'm ready, I recall thinking as I began reading. Let's fly.

Jones has been an abductee since age 5, he informs us. His earliest contacts were comforting, even exciting, only later during his teen years did he perceive them as scary, fearful, traumatic.

In the early contacts he received nighttime visits from a person he named "The Witch" because she could fly. He would see a point of light, then a ball of light. Then a being he perceived as female would be standing by his bed. She was skinny and he could not recognize a nose or mouth. She wore clothes that reminded him of a fish. She had four fingers, not five as he thought she should have.

Even as a child Jones knew the female being was real. She could talk to him.

"Can we be friends?" he asked her.

"We've always been friends," she replied.

Meeting with Little Star

At age 18, Jones awoke from a dream of flying. He becomes aware of a soft orange light. He is in a dome-shaped room with white walls which remind him of an igloo.

Seated across from him, cross-legged, is a child of about 4 or 5. She claps her hands and jabbers about flying and Peter Pan. Jones thinks of the nursery rhyme "Twinkle, Twinkle, Little Star" and names the child "Little Star."

Little Star plays with some blocks, makes them float and defy gravity. They talk for a while and then "The Witch" arrives, takes Little Star by the hand and Little Star takes Jones' hand. They go to another room, which Jones recognizes from previous visits. The child goes off with "The Witch" and Jones awakes in his bed at home.

On another occasion Jones describes the situation he finds himself in on one of the ships. He is laying on a table. Shadowy gray figures move about him in unison. He sits up. A tall figure appears. She asks him questions, "What do you want from us? What can we do for you?"

Jones: "I'm not afraid of you anymore."

Tall Being: "That was always your choice; at all times there was love."

After more conversation, Jones is returned to his home with a new understanding and possibly a new implant. His psychic awareness has been heightened. He understood more about ET contact. His fear was lessened or gone. One of the reasons Jones wrote his book, he tells us, is to show folks that they cannot only survive an abduction experience but flourish.

Jones begins speaking at conferences including Laughlin, Nevada.

Returning from the fabulous UFO Conference in Laughlin, Jones and his wife observe that their mail has been opened, their phone is tapped and a black helicopter flies low down their street and over their house—*whomp, whomp, whomp.* Big Brother has been at work, or perhaps the alien thought police are interfering.

Eventually Jones travels to New York City and contacts Budd Hopkins, the noted artist/abduction researcher. Hopkins interviews Jones, explores his memories and invites him to join his abduction therapy group. There Jones meets Linda Cortile, the subject of *Witnessed,* a book about her extraordinary abduction before multiple witnesses and United Nations officials. Jones, his wife Annie and Linda Cortile become close friends and share experiences and dinners.

Hopkins introduced Jones to John Mack, the Harvard psychiatrist and author of the seminal work *Abduction*, and to other notables in the field of ufology. (Sadly, both Mack and Hopkins have now passed on. Their contributions to ufology were enormous.) In time, Jones and Little Star meet on the Earth plane, face to face, but for that ongoing story folks will have to read the book.

Can You See Us Now?

Jones is a thoughtful guy who writes fluently about his experiences. This may be due in part to his achieving almost total recall of those experiences, a gift from his alien friends, he believes, around 2004.

In a 2009 encounter, he is driving around London. He hears and sees a black helicopter, low overhead. There are no markings or identification on it except for a shark-like nose pointed down toward his car and himself. The helicopter leaves. He drives on. It returns, then leaves again.

Jones drives on to visit a friend in rural London. He stops at the friend's house and goes to his trunk to get something. Turning, he bumps smack into a woman, possibly 7 feet tall.

"Still looking for those helicopters, are you?" She pushed on his forehead with three long fingers. "You can see us now, can't you?" She tells him it's time for him to wake up and remember. Then she's gone as Jones stands there pondering the encounter and not seeing her leave.

Paranormal Conference

There is a footnote to this short review of a long and detailed abduction life story.

In November 2011 Jones spoke at the Paranormal Conference in Taos, New Mexico. I was there in the second row with my skeptical buddy, Philip. Jones related a few stories from his book, most of which I was familiar with. After he finished, I nudged Philip. "What did you think?"

Without hesitation Philip said, "It's all B.S., Jim. There's no documentation for any of it."

"I don't think they welcome cameras on the ships," I said quietly. "This is the real deal!"

Jones spoke again a few days later; a few of his comments and those from the book may have merged in my mind.

The Light Beings

He talked (or wrote) how his contacts changed and evolved over time. He still sees the Grays but he also sees a race which he calls The Light Beings. They look more like us and apparently don't abduct people. He forms a question in his mind and they answer it.

Would aliens fly billions of miles just to help our planet and warn us of atomic and environmental dangers?

"Yes," Jones says, and he cites the theory in quantum physics that we are all connected, as a basis for their concern.

He also comments that some aliens may dwell in a dimension or frequency that is nearby and may not require extensive travel.

"They are not here to hurt us. They are positive," Jones believes. "Fear the manipulating humans," he said, "not the sky travelers."

For those who want to learn more about aliens, this is the latest book. Informative and fascinating, it belongs alongside *Abduction* by Mack, and *Missing Time, Intruders*, and *Witnessed* by Hopkins.

It is a must read for those troubled by the alien presence.

Chapter 5

'Witness to Roswell' Uncovers Cover-up

"These people will kill you if I tell you what I know."
— Mac Brazel to Roswell newsman Bob Wolf,
shortly before Brazel died

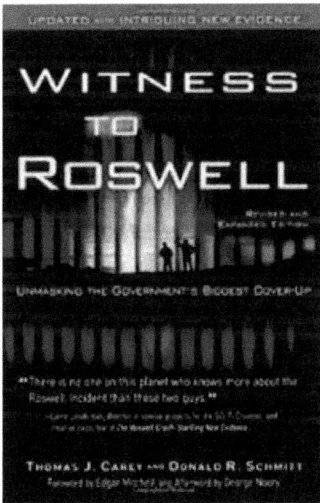

Finally, a detailed and well-documented book about the Roswell Incident and cover-up. No longer will researchers of the Incident have to argue over the exact location of the three crash sites, the nature of the military cover-up, the personnel involved, or the size and shape of the crash vehicle and bodies.

These issues have now been settled by the eyewitness death-bed testimony of none other than Walter Haut, co-founder of the Roswell UFO Museum and Research Center, and by other witnesses.

For years Haut maintained that all he ever did (or saw) was to deliver the press release announcing the

recovery of "a flying disc"—the shot heard round the world
—to the four Roswell news outlets. Acting on authority of
his boss, Colonel Blanchard, Haut personally conveyed
Blanchard's dictated words to the media.

Now we learn from Haut's testimony—signed,
witnessed and dated December 26, 2002—that Haut
attended a secret meeting at 7:30 a.m. on July 8, 1947 at
the Roswell Army Air Base. Present were General Roger
Ramey, commander, Eighth Air Force, Fort Worth,
Texas, his deputy, Col. Duboise, Col. Blanchard (RAAF)
and air staff officers, and Haut.

Debris from the crash site was passed around and
discussed while General Ramey outlined a cover-up
proposal (which Haut believed Ramey had received from
the Pentagon).

Later that morning, Col. Blanchard took Haut to
Hangar 84, the B29 hangar on the eastern edge of the
runway (then building P-3). There, under high security,
Haut saw the heads of crash victim bodies which he
described as "larger than normal" and the bodies under
tarp "the size of a ten-year-old child." Haut also saw the
crash vehicle which he described as "6 ft. in height, 12-
15 ft. in length," "egg-shaped" and "metallic," without
windows, portholes, wings, tail section, or landing gear.
"What I observed," Haut stated in paragraph 19 of his
declaration, "was some type of craft and its crew from
outer space."

Haut also described how Major Marcel, base
intelligence officer, flew with some crates to Carswell
Army Air Base (Fort Worth, Texas) and took debris from
the crash site to General Ramey. Major Marcel, however,
told Haut that Ramey substituted a weather balloon
for the debris Marcel had carried there. From other
interviews, authors Carey and Schmitt learned that

a second B29 made an unscheduled secret flight with bodies and craft vehicle to Wright Field in Ohio (now Wright Patterson AFB).

Over many years, authors Carey and Schmitt interviewed numerous witnesses to important aspects of this case. These interviews are summarized in the book, especially concerning the location and cleanup of the three sites—the Brazel debris site on the ranch he managed, the bodies at a location a few miles away, and the site northwest of Roswell where the craft crash-landed. All three sites were under heavy security, and personnel who knew what had happened were sworn to secrecy using intimidation and National Security Laws.

Hangar 84 in Roswell

There are at least two more key witnesses to the Roswell Incident whose testimony is new and almost as important as Haut's.

Mac Brazel, the rancher who first reported the debris field and brought debris ito Roswell on July 6,

1947, held several conversations with Roswell newsman Frank Joyce. For years Joyce stated that Brazel talked only about the debris field on the ranch which he (Brazel) managed. Something unusual crashed there.

Then, in 1998, the authors of *Witness* interviewed Joyce. Joyce had just retired from his Albuquerque news job with station KOB. Joyce stated that Brazel told him on July 6, 1947 that Brazel had seen "bodies," "little people," "creatures" on the ground a few miles south of the debris field.

Joyce decided to play devil's advocate. He told Brazel that perhaps he had seen monkeys which the military had been sending into space. Before Brazel slammed down the phone, he shouted, "Dammit, they're not monkeys and they're not human."

Walter Haut's testimony was made public in July 2007 upon the publication of *Witness to Roswell* at the UFO Museum in Roswell, with a book signing for authors Carey and Schmitt. Many UFO researchers, including this writer, believe this book proves that a space craft crashed at Roswell in July 1947.

This photo shows a UFO flying over Phoenix on July 7, 1947. The photographer, William Rhodes, was interviewed by the FBI and later invited to Wright Patterson AFB (then Wright Field) to discuss his sighting. The flying object is similar to the description given by Walter Haut in his deathbed testament of the craft which crashed near Roswell in 1947. Haut was co-founder of the Roswell UFO Museum. Near the end of his life, he stated he had seen bodies and a "spacecraft" at the Roswell Army air field in 1947, according to *Witness to Roswell*. **Photo courtesy Carol Syska, former director of the Roswell UFO Museum and Research Center, and James Parsons.**

Chapter 6

Credit the aliens for modern-day technology

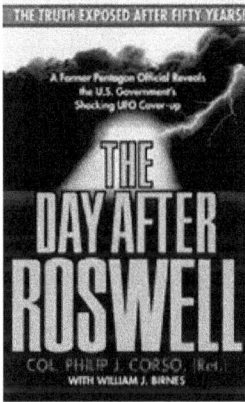

The Day After Roswell
by Colonel Philip J. Corso, Retired,
with William J. Birnes (1998)
978-0-671017-56-9
Pocket Books

Finally, a book about the reality of the UFO crash at Roswell from a high-ranking military man in the know.

Corso, President Eisenhower's military liaison and a member of the National Security Council in the 1950s, has not only confirmed that an alien space craft and bodies were recovered at Roswell in 1947, but he relates how he participated in a "reverse engineering" program to make recovered alien technology available to U.S. industry.

In 1961, Corso was assigned to Research and Development (R&D) at the Pentagon, working under Lt. General Arthur Trudeau, head of Army R&D. According to Corso, Trudeau placed the Army's Roswell crash materials in Corso's hands and directed Corso to feed information learned from the Roswell crash to selected arms industries.

For the next two years, without disclosing his source of information, Corso says he gave selected U.S. defense contractors discoveries related to night-vision viewers, bulletproof vests, integrated circuit chip technology, fiber optics and lasers.

Author Corso writes that the design of America's Stealth aircraft was a direct result of studies made of the Roswell crash vehicle. The skin of the Stealth, which conceals it from enemy radar and heat-seeking missiles, is also a direct result of these studies of the UFO, Corso says.

In his book, Corso names experts, scientists and companies associated with this amazing tale. In an aside, he comments that the Roswell saucer is now housed in a top-secret kind of "alien technology museum" at Norton Air Force Base in California.

Corso explains the extreme secrecy which has surrounded the subject of UFOs for 50 years. According to him, the CIA was known by Army Intelligence to have been infiltrated by the KGB. "The only way to keep the UFO secrets from the Russians was to keep them secret from ourselves," Corso writes. Only a few high-placed individuals would be told the truth about aliens and UFOs. So secret was the subject that even presidents subsequent to Eisenhower were excluded from the knowledge, Corso writes. Officially, "nobody knew anything and nothing happened."

The architect of the secrecy plan known as MJ-12, according to Corso, was General Nathan Twining. General Twining is known by researchers to have flown to Roswell shortly after the crash in his capacity as head of Air Materiel Command and Scientific Labs. Later Twining became chief of the joint chiefs. "Deny everything," Corso quotes Twining as having said to President Truman, "but let public sentiment take its course."

Successors to the original MJ-12 people still exist, according to Corso, and are now known simply as the "UFO Working Group." However, those in the know serve in various government departments and are no longer a unified group. Those who are shown the secrets are immediately bound by National Security legislation and cannot reveal what they have been shown, according to Corso.

In Chapter 2, Corso relates how he, as a young night-duty officer at Fort Riley, Kansas, obtained an unauthorized peek at an alien body. This happened on July 6, 1947, Corso wrote, two days after the crash at Roswell.

At a book and author event in Albuquerque, Corso told friends of this reviewer that he would provide documentation for his claims at a later time. At present all documents and records remain classified.

No book of this detail and scope from an insider has ever been written about the Roswell case. In this reviewer's opinion, a decision has been made at a very high level to allow UFO information to leak to the public in the 1990s.

A Memorial Tribute to Philip Corso

Col. Philip J. Corso, retired from the U.S. Army, and author of *The Day After Roswell,* passed on in July 1998. This review, which appeared in the November 1997 issue of *The Star Beacon,* is reprinted here in memory of a man dedicated to revealing the truth about what happened at Roswell in July 1947.

A New World IF You Can Take It

Researcher Paola Harris came up with a great story when she interviewed Colonel Philip J. Corso in 1997 at the 50th anniversary of the Roswell crash of 1947. Harris released this story to the public on the Internet recently and I have summarized it below.

Here's the story:

After leaving his job as military liaison to President Eisenhower in 1957, Ike gave Corso a coveted job as Brigade Missile Commander at White Sands Proving Ground (now White Sands Missile Range), New Mexico. It should be noted that White Sands is a huge military reservation in southern New Mexico. For some reason unspecified, Corso found himself driving to an abandoned gold mine which was located on the base. Corso entered the mine and—much to his surprise—he encountered an alien being there.

Dressed in a space suit, the alien wore a glass helmet with a silverfish band and a red jewel or sensor in the center. The alien had a request of the Colonel. He asked Corso to shut down the radars on the base for ten minutes. "Now how did he know that I was the only person that could give such an order?" Corso said to Harris.

And what will you give me in return? Corso asked. "A new world, if you can take it," the alien said.

Returning to his Jeep, Corso called range headquarters and ordered the radar officer to shut down the radars for 10 minutes. Then, seeing the alien at the mine entrance,

Corso gave the alien a salute.

Returning to base, Corso learned a UFO was leaving the area at 3,000-4,000 mph. In his mind, Corso heard the words, "I return your salute." *Was this thing a soldier too?* Corso wondered aloud.

A fine story, thanks to Paola Harris and Corso's son on *Coast to Coast.*

Chapter 7

Jackie Gleason's trip to the alien morgue

By **Marty Murray**

MORTYSCABIN.NET

"To the moon, Alice!"

There was a time when you could say that phrase and immediately most everyone knew exactly who you're talking about: "The Great One."

The fine actor and comedian Jackie Gleason will forever be associated with his role of bus driver Ralph Cramden on the popular TV series, *The Honeymooners*. But there was another side to Jackie that few people know about. Gleason was an extremely serious armchair UFO researcher, and prided himself on his huge collection of UFO-related books, which numbered into the thousands.

As soon as a new title came out, even in Europe or the UK, Jackie had a copy. Little did he suspect that his interest in that topic would one day gain him access to something that most people would never even believe, and would leave others who shared his interests either skeptical or forever jealous.

It was a chance conversation one afternoon, back in 1974 in Florida, while Jackie was playing golf with one of his regular partners, President Richard Nixon. Jackie had mentioned his interest in UFOs and his large collection of books, and the President admitted that he also shared Jackie's interest and had a sizeable collection of UFO-oriented materials of his own. At the time, the President said little about what he actually knew, but things were to change drastically later on that same night.

One can only imagine Gleason's surprise when President Nixon showed up at his house around midnight, completely alone and driving his own private car. When Jackie asked him why he was there, Nixon told him that he wanted to take him somewhere and show him something. He got into the President's car, and they ended up at the gates of Homestead Air Force Base. They passed through security and drove to the far end of the base, to a tightly guarded building. At this point, I will quote directly from Gleason himself, from an interview he gave to UFO researcher and author Larry Warren:

"We drove to the very far end of the base in a segregated area, finally stopping near a well-guarded building. The security police saw us coming and just sort of moved back as we passed them and entered the structure. There were a number of labs we passed through first before we entered a section where Nixon pointed out what he said was the wreckage from a flying saucer, enclosed in several large cases. Next, we went into an inner chamber and there were six or eight of what looked like glass-topped Coke freezers. Inside them were the mangled remains of what I took to be children. Then—upon closer examination—I saw that some of the other figures looked quite old. Most of them were terribly mangled as if they had been in an accident."

Gleason was understandably excited by all of this, but also quite traumatized, and said he couldn't eat or sleep properly for weeks afterwards, and found himself drinking heavily until he was able to regain his composure. His wife at the time, Beverly, recalls him being out very late that night and speaking excitedly about what he had seen when he returned home.

Later on, however, when she and Gleason were splitting up and she told the story to a writer at *Esquire Magazine*, which printed it in an article, relations between her and the entertainer deteriorated and Gleason became very upset and angry that the story had been made public.

For this reason many people, including Beverly herself, have wondered at the truth of the story. However, in his interview with Larry Warren, who was invited to Jackie's house in person because Gleason wanted to hear firsthand about Warren's experience at Bentwaters Air Force Base in England, it was clear that Jackie was being honest and sincere:

"You could tell that he was very sincere—he took the whole affair very seriously, and I could tell that he wanted to get the matter off his chest, and that was why he was telling me all of this. Jackie felt just like I do, that the government needs to 'come clean,' and tell us all it knows about space visitors. It's time they stopped lying to the public and release all the evidence they have. When they do, then we'll all be able to see the same things the late Jackie Gleason did."

The United States government's knowledge about UFOs and their occupants exists at the very highest levels of security, above even atomic weapons and things of that nature. Information is imparted on a strictly "need to know" basis, and this has left even many presidents in the dark on the subject.

Obviously, Richard Nixon wasn't one of them. One

can only imagine what technology and evidence of life outside of this Earth exists in the back corners and hidden labs of the American military, but for anyone who doesn't believe that this situation is real, this story about Jackie Gleason is just the very tiny tip of the iceberg. We may be waiting a very, very long time, indeed, until Jackie's dream of government disclosure comes true.

Chapter 8

Operation Majestic-12

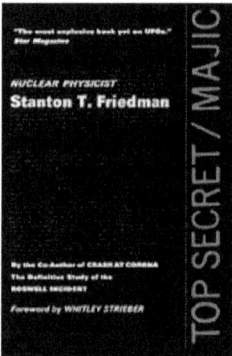

Top Secret/MAJIC, Stanton Friedman (1996)

The UFO Book, Jerome Clark (1998)

The Day After Roswell, Philip J. Corso (1997)

In the legend, lore and history of flying saucers, no area of study has become more controversial than the Majestic-12 documents. Long before the documents surfaced, UFO researchers suspected that a secret group of high-placed individuals controlled almost every aspect of UFO information and its release. Those of us weaned on the books by Major Donald Keyhoe (*Flying Saucers Are Real,* 1950; *Flying Saucers From Outer Space,* 1960; *Flying Saucer Conspiracy,* 1955, and *Flying Saucers: Top Secret,* 1960) recall his theory that the "silence group"— or some such association of elitist men—were guilty of lies and disinformation about UFOs to an uninformed and unsuspecting public.

Comes then in 1984 a roll of 35 mm black and white film mailed anonymously to researcher Jaime Shandera in California. When the film is developed, researchers are surprised to view briefing documents dated 1952 and labeled, "TOP SECRET / MAJIC EYES ONLY" for President-Elect Eisenhower. The documents describe the crash of two alien spacecraft—the Roswell crash in particular—the cover-up and alien bodies recovered and held for scientific study. Further, the documents listed a group of high government, military and scientific men— 12 in all—who would oversee the entire business of crashed saucers, keeping it secret and acting on authority from President Harry Truman. Truman's letter, dated September 24, 1947, to Secretary of Defense Forrestal, establishing Majestic-12, is one of the documents for President-Elect Eisenhower's eyes only.

The Majestic-12 documents are dynamite in the UFO field, if true, but are they genuine? Stanton Friedman, tireless researcher of the Roswell Incident and book with that title and author of *Top Secret/MAJIC*, took up the challenge of authentication.

Physicist Friedman, in a methodical manner, sifted through thousands of documents at 15 government archives and libraries, focusing on correspondence to and by Truman, Eisenhower, Marshall, Forrestal, Twining, Hillenkoetter and anything mentioning Majestic-12. Friedman and the archivists compared elements of the MJ-12 documents—typefaces, data formats, signatures, security markings, etc.—with substantiated and verified letters and documents in the archives. Friedman interviewed senior archivists, widows of Majestic-12 listed members and executive secretaries of the 12 individuals (all 12 were deceased at the time of the release of Majestic-12 documents).

Friedman discovered that the 12 listed Majestic-12 members were logical choices to be involved. Six were civilian, six military, one (Vannevar Bush) a distinguished scientist and science advisor to Harry Truman, another Truman's Secretary of Defense, another Director of the CIA, and so on down the list. In his book, Friedman answers challenges to the documents from "nay sayers" and leading "debunkers."

A disputed date format on the documents (18 November, 1952) was found by Friedman to be in use on other top secret documents of unimpeachable provenance and of the period. One document which surfaced after the others was signed by Harry Truman with only his first name, "Harry." Did Truman ever sign with only his first name? A letter was signed "approved Harry Truman" in script. The signature was challenged. Friedman found examples of both signatures on other verified documents, although "Harry" was usually reserved for personal correspondence.

Several of the senior document people Friedman consulted with told him they had no reason to doubt the authenticity of the documents. One senior archivist commented he would be unable to fake the documents because of the extreme detail and inside information required to make a believable fake.

During Friedman's research, more Majestic documents surfaced anonymously. A 22-page technical manual, titled "Extraterrestrial Entities and Technology, Recovery and Disposal," is fascinating to read by this reviewer, who was a technical writer of government aerospace manuals in the late 1950s. The technical manual, reproduced in Friedman's book, details how to package crashed saucers and bodies, where to ship them, security level required for all handlers—Majic Eyes Only clearance, two levels above top secret—and what to do with living organisms—live aliens. An amazing document still under evaluation by researchers.

Friedman's book is a fabulous detective story and more. Its story will result in a changed world cosmology and consciousness when it is understood and assimilated by the public.

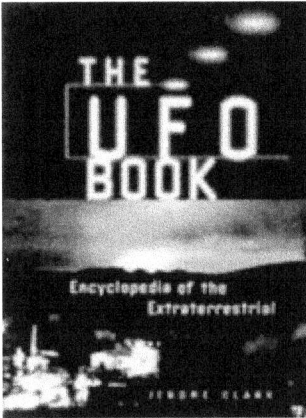

N ow about *The UFO Book* (1998) by Jerome Clark. Based on a three-volume encyclopedia of UFO information edited by Clark, this book is a readable and informative summary of the whole UFO field—no small accomplishment. A celebrated whitewash case, known as the *Condon Report*, is beautifully presented in the book. Leading UFO researchers of past years, such as Donald Keyhoe, are fairly profiled. Clark relates how Major Keyhoe "blasted" those in high places who controlled the free flow of information about UFOs and how he (Keyhoe) was continuously a thorn in the side of the military.

Keyhoe charged in the 1950s that the Air Force knew UFOs were coming from outer space, but intentionally played down important cases, proposed phony explanations for valid sightings, and hid the most sensitive cases. Information to the public was to be released "slowly," according to Keyhoe in *The UFO Book,* so that the public would be prepared when the whole story came out.

But *The UFO Book* contains serious omissions and flaws, in the opinion of this reviewer. For one, to dismiss the Billy Meier case in one sentence, labeling it a fraud, is inexcusable. The old pilots, physicists, writers and photo experts who have studied this case have flown to

Switzerland to discuss the case endlessly with Meier and associates, looked at landing tracks, examined thousands of photographs, film and negatives and consulted many specialists to reach their favorable opinion. Further, the spaceships photographed by Meier have been seen and photographed by other witnesses in various parts of the earth over the years. Clark should, at the very least, keep an open mind about this important case.

Secondly, Clark describes the Majestic-12 documents as "unrestrained paranoia" portraying in his introduction a "nightmarish vision of a malevolent Washington," and he labels the documents a hoax. His view of the Majestic-12 documents is unsubstantiated in *The UFO Book*, and Friedman's enormous contribution to ufology is largely ignored. He lists Friedman's book in his bibliography, so he must have read it. Perhaps he should read it again.

Thirdly, in Clark's book there is no mention of my hero, Philip Corso (*The Day After Roswell,* 1997). How can any survey of the UFO field done in 1998 ignore Corso? Corso, in his book and recorded interviews, explained that the original Majestic-12 group, after its inception in the late 1940s, began to change in the 1950s. By the middle of the Eisenhower years, seams opened up in "the grand camouflage scheme." The cover-up became covered up from the cover-up, Corso wrote, "leaving the few of us in-the-know free to do what we wanted." Then Corso went on to explain how some of the technology recovered at Roswell was infused and

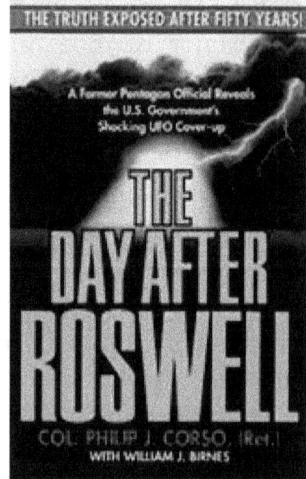

and back-engineered into high-tech weaponry.

Successors to the old MJ-12, according to Corso, continue to serve in various government agencies, but with lesser control over the subject (UFOs). It is one or more of these successors that this reviewer believes released the Majestic-12 documents intentionally, because it is time for this information to come forth. The importance of these documents is that they partially explain what has been happening with UFOs and why for over 50 years.

Over and over Corso said, "Tell the youth, tell your grandchildren. They have a right to know."

Since writing the article on Majestic-12, the reviewer has learned that new documents have surfaced. Dr. Robert Wood and his son, Ryan, have undertaken the task of authentication of both old and new documents. At a major address before the International UFO Congress in Laughlin, Nevada, last February (1999), Ryan Wood told us that the new documents, as well as the old, appear to be authentic. Every objection of the "nay sayers" is being addressed. (*See Appendix*.) You can order a complete text of the documents from Wood & Wood Enterprises, P.O. Box 2272, Redwood City, CA 94064-2272.

Chapter 9

Crash at Roswell
The Los Alamos Connection

A visit to the International UFO Museum at Roswell, New Mexico, would lead one to believe that the alleged crash of a UFO near that city in July 1947 was a true extraterrestrial event. At least six alternating videos and numerous displays and audio tapes explore testimony from eyewitnesses and strong circumstantial evidence of an alien crash, recovery and its cover-up by higher military authorities.

Several of the pilots at the Roswell Army Air Force Base at the time state on tape that within a few days of the incident they flew wreckage to Fort Worth Army Air Field, to Washington, D.C., and to Wright Field (Dayton, Ohio). Three flights were also made to Los Alamos, New Mexico. Of course these unscheduled flights said to be hauling crash debris do not prove that an extraterrestrial vehicle was recovered or covered up at Roswell. What the flights prove is that the crash was taken seriously by the Base commander at Roswell and his intelligence and air staffs at the local level.

Comes now a story out of Roswell and Los Alamos which may explain the three flights made from Roswell

Army Air Field to Los Alamos on July 9, 1947, a few days after the crash. This story is from Carol Syska, former director of the UFO Museum at Roswell during 1999 and most of 2000.

Carol was a group secretary and division budget director at Los Alamos for almost 30 years. She retired in 1988 and moved to Roswell, New Mexico, not far from the town where she was born and raised. Carol first heard of UFOs when living in California in the early 1950s, resulting in an interest in UFOs in general.

One day at Los Alamos, she read that a report containing information about UFOs was available in the Lab library. This sounded interesting to Carol. She ordered the report. She read this booklet, titled "Project Blue Book," which contained some comments about wreckage from a crashed vehicle being sent for testing to Los Alamos.

At the time (1962), Carol worked at the Lab with the NonDestructive Test Group (NDT). Her boss, a senior scientist, was head of NDT and had been with the Lab since the beginning of the Manhattan Project. If testing had been done on crash debris, Carol's boss would know about the tests and the truth of the crash at Roswell.

Carol went to the man's office and showed the report to him. She asked, "Is this true?"

Carol's boss, in a business-like manner, replied, "What is the level of your security clearance?"

Carol said, "Sir, you know as well as I do what it is." (Carol told me that at the time she held a Q clearance. A Q clearance is a very high National Security clearance.)

Carol's boss, after a pause, said, "Well, do you have the need to know?"

Carol said, "Guess not," and moved to the door.

Carol's boss said, "Just a minute." After another

pause, he added, "I would advise you to read everything you ever see about this subject."

That was the end of the conversation. Carol never discussed the matter again with her supervisor, the senior scientist, who is now deceased. But Carol believes the scientist gave her a glimpse of the truth.

Chapter 10

Tribute to Neil Armstrong

On July 20, 1969, as Commander of the Apollo 11 lunar module, astronaut Neil Armstrong was the first person to set foot on the Moon. His first words after stepping onto the Moon's surface were: "That's one small step for man, one giant leap for mankind," and those words were televised to the people on Earth.

Just before Neil re-entered the Lander, he made this remark: "Good luck, Mr. Gorsky." Many people at NASA thought that was just a casual remark concerning some rival Soviet cosmonaut. However, there was no Mr. Gorsky in either the Russian nor American space programs.

Over the years many people questioned Armstrong about his statement, "Good luck, Mr. Gorsky," but Neil would only smile.

On July 5, 1995 in Tampa Bay, Florida, following a speech, a reporter brought up the 26-year-old question, and Armstrong finally responded. Mr. Gorsky had died, so Neil felt he could finally answer.

In 1938, when he was a kid in a small Midwestern town, he was playing baseball with a friend in the backyard and his friend hit the ball, which landed in his neighbor's yard next to their bedroom window. As Neil leaned down to pick up the ball, he heard Mrs. Gorsky shouting at her Mr. Gorsky: "Sex! You want sex? You'll get sex when the kid next door walks on the Moon!"

Neil Armstrong made his transition on August 25, 2012 at the age of 82.

Neil Armstrong's UFO Secret

Dr. Steven Greer wrote the following, which appeared on Dr. Greer's blog at the Disclosure Project Web site:

"Many have asked if Armstrong took with him the secrets of what really happened during the famed 1969 Lunar Landing. Well, yes—and no.

"Over the years, I have gotten to know a number of astronauts—and very close family members and friends of astronauts. As you may recall, my uncle was the senior project engineer for Grumman (now Northrop Grumman) that built the Lunar Module, that landed on the moon in July of 1969.

"The truth of that historic event has never been told. We did go to the Moon—but the events that transpired were kept secret and officially remain secret to this day.

"By the time we landed on the Moon, the Lunar Orbiter had mapped the Moon and imaged ancient as well as more recent structures on the Moon. This has been confirmed by more than one Disclosure Project witness. So by the time we landed, the military and intelligence community—and a small compartment of operatives at NASA—knew that we may in fact encounter something very unusual there.

"To prepare for this possibility, there was a time delay from the Lunar Module via an NSA (National Security Agency) uplink and other, alternative film footage was prepared to be shown in the event of something really unusual happening.

"Well, it happened. Close friends and very close family members of both Neil Armstrong and Buzz Aldrin have separately told me that indeed there were numerous, large UFOs around the crater where the Lunar Module landed and that these were seen by both Armstrong and Aldrin. I have also spoken to military officers that have seen the footage of this event—but it has never been made public. One close family member of Buzz Aldrin told me: "It is not my place to out Buzz on this—someday if he can speak about it, he will ..."

"Neil Armstrong became somewhat of a recluse after the moon landing, and rarely spoke of the historic event. His friends and family have told me that this is because he was a man of such integrity that he simply did not want to be put in a position to lie to the public about such a momentous encounter. How tragic that our heroes have been placed in this untenable situation!

"When we were organizing the Disclosure Project a few years ago, I asked one of Neil Armstrong's friends if Armstrong would come to Washington to brief members of Congress at the 1997 Congressional briefing we organized in April of that year. I was told that Armstrong wished he could—but that if he spoke about what really happened during the moon landing, that Neil Armstrong, his wife, and children would all be killed. It was put to me this bluntly.

"I found this to be unbelievable at the time, but since then have found that such threats and bullying by the over-reaching national security state is routine. A very senior scientist at the Naval Research Labs in Washington, DC, recently told me and the Disclosure Project team that if he spoke about some of the information he knew, that he, his wife, his children and grandchildren would all be killed.

73

"This is no joke—and not a conspiracy theory. This is the way the highly secretive and fascist bosses in the deep black national security state operate. They make the Mafia look like choir boys.

"In the meanwhile, we continue to applaud those courageous men and women who come forward, speak the truth and move Disclosure forward. The world deserves to know that we are not alone, that intelligent life exists in the universe beyond Earth and that we have amazing new sciences and technologies that urgently need to be disclosed. This knowledge will give us a new civilization on Earth, without poverty or pollution—and with justice for all.

"The upcoming film *Sirius* will advance this cause—and it must. Please help us in this endeavor. Go to Sirius, *Neverendinglight.com,* and join the thousands who are supporting the next big step in Disclosure, Peaceful Contact and New Energy."

Chapter 11

Captured! The True Story of the World's First Documented Alien Abduction

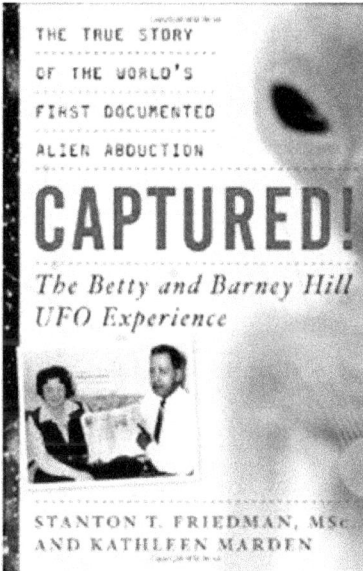

Captured! The True Story of the World's First Documented Alien Abduction, The Betty and Barney Hill UFO Experience, Stanton T. Friedman, MSc, and Kathleen Marden ISBN 1-56414-971-4 Career Press, Franklin Lakes, New Jersey, August 2007

Guest Review by **Ann Miller**

One book crossed my path on its way to my son, who reviews books for *The Star Beacon,* that I couldn't resist reading myself. It's destined to be a blockbuster in the UFO field, since it is all about the first documented UFO abduction in ufological history, the famous Betty and Barney Hill incident of September 19-20, 1961, in the White Mountains of New Hampshire.

I remember when I first read about Betty and Barney Hill in the mid '60s—how intriguing a story it was—especially at that time. It was especially memorable to me, since its knowledge came to me at a time when I'd started having sightings of my own, but on a much smaller scale, obviously.

Everyone in the UFO community knows of Stanton Friedman, who is a nuclear physicist, and since 1967 has lectured on the topic, "Flying Saucers ARE Real!" at more than 600 colleges and more than 100 professional groups in 50 states, nine provinces and 16 other countries. He's published more than 80 UFO papers and has appeared on hundreds of radio and TV programs. Friedman is the original civilian investigator of the Roswell Incident, and co-authored *Crash at Corona: The Definitive Study of the Roswell Incident,* and authored *Top Secret / Majic: Operation Majestic-12 and the United States Government's UFO Cover-Up.*

Kathleen Marden is Betty Hill's niece, and also a trained social scientist and educator who has served on the MUFON Board of Directors. She was 13 on the day Betty called her mother (Betty's sister) to report that the previous evening she and Barney had encountered a flying saucer in New Hampshire's White Mountains. As a primary witness to the evidence and aftermath, Kathleen has intimate knowledge of the Hills' biographical histories, personalities and never-before-published historical data that pertains to their sensational story.

Captured! reveals to the public for the first time the eyewitness scenes of the Hills' extraordinary encounter with the massive space vehicle and eleven alien figures, plus interviews with U.S. Air Force officials, a comparative analysis of the fascinating hypnosis sessions that exposed the terrifying onboard experiences of the abductees, the physical and social characteristics of the aliens, scientific interest, and the controversy that followed.

Now, 46 years after the Hills' abduction, more people than ever are convinced that UFOs are real and have been covered up by the government. Friedman and Marden turn up riveting interview transcripts and tapes, and military, medical and psychiatric reports. After decades of research and work with scientists and organizations dedicated to collecting and analyzing UFO data, they have produced this book which will keep you rooted to your seat as you read the definitive and dramatic portrayal of the enigmatic incident and its consequences.

The book is a collector's item for your library of esoteric reading. It contains old pictures and illustrations of interest, as well as sidebar-type mini-biographies of certain investigators involved in the case. And it is presented in such a way that you'll be able to make up your own mind what you believe about this startlingly famous UFO case.

Chapter 12

Secrets, Truth and Destiny

"Try to understand. This is for your world as well as for ours."   *— Alien to Elizabeth Robinson*

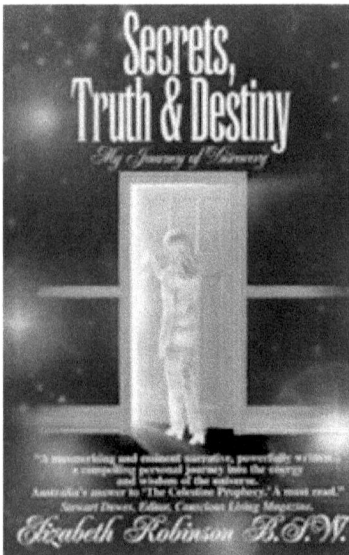

Secrets, Truth and Destiny, My Journey of Discovery, Elizabeth Robinson
ISBN 978-0646351339
Key Publishing (Australia), 1997

In a field fraught with strange occurrences and tales, perhaps strangest of all is the abduction scenario as reported by those who say they have been taken aboard UFOs and have undergone medical examinations as well as interaction with an alien race. The following is a portion of the story and a review of what is known and believed to be true by researchers who study abductions today.

The usual starting point of abduction tales is the case of Betty and Barney Hill. The Hills, under hypnosis, talked of being taken from their automobile near the White Mountains of New Hampshire in 1961. They told of being teleported into a hovering spacecraft and given what they believed were medical exams. Later they were returned to their auto. A newspaper man wrote a best-selling book about the case, *The Interrupted Journey*, subsequently presented as a story televised to a large audience.

Later studies of people who believed they had undergone an alien abduction produced more detailed information about a vast genetic program being conducted in the skies above Earth. A university professor by the name of David Jacobs, at Temple University in Pennsylvania, studied 300 cases of reported abductions and published his findings in a book called *Secret Life* (1992). Jacobs' research was supported by the abduction research of John Mack, a Harvard University professor, in his book *Abduction* (1994).

These books confirmed the prior research done by artist Budd Hopkins in *Missing Time* and *Intruders,* and the personal experiences of Whitley Strieber in his best-selling book *Communion*. These researchers heard hundreds of abductees under hypnosis relate how they had been teleported against their will into spaceships, stripped, placed on tables and underwent invasive medical procedures.

Many of the abductees related how they were a part of a larger program which would result in a new race of people now known as "hybrids," part human and part alien. After the publication of *Communion*, Strieber received 200,000 compelling letters from people who believed they had had experiences similar to his. Some of these letters are related in *Communion Letters* (1997).

Jacobs and other researchers were told by those

interviewed that the alien abductors were beings small in stature, 3 ½ to 5 feet in height, gray in color with large almond-shaped eyes and four fingers on each hand, with no thumb, according to one eyewitness, the nurse who drew pictures of the hands for Glenn Dennis, chairman, Roswell UFO Museum.

The race of little beings has become known as "The Grays." According to many reports, the Grays communicate mentally with each other and with the abductees rather than using spoken language. Many reports say an alien referred to as "A Taller Being" is generally present, participates in medical procedures and appears to be in charge.

Sounds like science fantasy, doesn't it? But, is it?

One of the newer speakers at UFO conferences is an Australian woman by the name of Elizabeth Robinson, herself an abductee and author of *Secrets, Truth and Destiny* (1997). Robinson told her abductors she wanted full recall if they were going to continue to take her and her daughter without her permission. According to Robinson, she has been granted partial recall and states that her abductors told her she is being prepared by several alien races to speak publicly about her experiences. Slowly and painfully Robinson has learned to overcome her fear of aliens.

"Try to understand," Robinson was told on the ships. "This is for your world as well as for ours. You are killing yourselves, and the result will be that you won't have an Earth to live on. You are polluting your world and not honoring your plant and animal kingdoms."

According to Robinson, she was taken aboard a larger ship, where she was shown incubators, infants, nurseries and playrooms where strange-looking children were housed. (Other abductees had this same experience.)

"These are your children," Robinson said she was told, and she was encouraged to interact with the children.

Robinson says in her book that the aliens are trying to impart a greater consciousness and understanding to the human race. One night, aboard a ship, she had a vision of dying fish washing up on Earth's shore. "It's not just pollution," she told us at a conference in Laughlin, Nevada, February 1999. "People are disconnected from Spirit, and Earth is crying out for help."

By the late 1990s, Robinson learned to let go of fear and the concept of good aliens and bad aliens. "We on Earth are as much alien or cosmic beings as those we refer to as alien," she wrote. "Our world is sacred and so are we. It is time for all of us to realize how incredibly special each one of us is, to see and honor the God in each other, to love and accept ourselves and one another … so that we can begin to take back our rightful place as members of the greater universe."

There is much more to the unfolding abduction story. If you are interested, the books are available.

Chapter 13

Mercury Astronaut Gordon Cooper
A True Hero

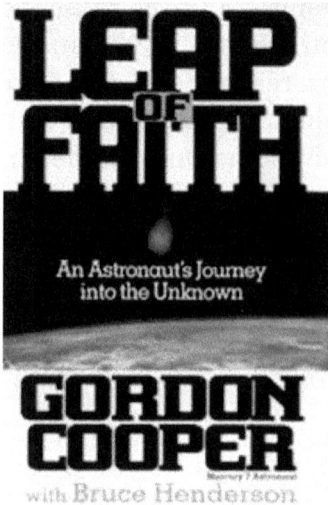

*Leap of Faith,
An Astronaut's Journey
into the Unknown*
Gordon Cooper and
Bruce Henderson
(2000)

For some men a life of high adventure is standard operating procedure. Gordon Cooper, retired Air Force colonel and pilot-astronaut of *Mercury 7* and *Gemini 5* space craft, is one of these men.

All of the *Mercury 7* astronauts risked their lives in space craft which, by today's standards, would be considered primitive and unsafe. Hence, in the early days of the space program, the astronauts pushed NASA for manual control—something NASA higher-ups resisted. Cooper spent considerable time in the simulator practicing re-entry, just in case there was an in-flight emergency. His extra hours proved well spent, because his first flight into space (in *Mercury 7*) was plagued with difficulties. One electrical system after another shut down until only the battery-operated communication channel was functional. It is exciting to read Cooper's account of how he coped with the crisis and manually piloted the craft safely back to Earth, landing almost on top of the rescue carrier *Kearsarge*.

But this is a review for students of UFOs. What we want to hear from Cooper are his own experiences with UFOs, which he describes in detail and forthrightly.

To begin with, Cooper states in Chapter Four that he did not see UFOs in space. Further, he states that he does not believe Armstrong and Aldrin saw UFOs on the Moon, even though statements to the contrary are found on the Internet. The only possible sighting by astronauts in space, Cooper states, is the "weird-looking object" sighted by McDivitt and White in *Gemini 4* over Hawaii.

Other sightings Cooper tells us about in his book are these: In 1951, as an F86 pilot in West Germany, he saw flights of UFOs traveling from east to west over Germany. He and the other pilots were ordered up to investigate. The UFOs were "metallic silver and saucer-shaped." They passed high above the ceiling altitude of the F86 at tremendous speeds, sometimes stopping in mid-air, hovering, then taking off at speeds beyond Earth aircraft capabilities. Sometimes the pilots watched the flights through binoculars from the ground. So common were these occurrences that in time the base no longer ordered the pilots up to investigate.

The next sighting Cooper describes occurred in 1957, when he was a test pilot at Edwards Air Force Base in California. Cooper's film crew (two enlisted personnel) were on the edge of the base filming a precision landing system. A "strange-looking saucer" flew over, hovered above ground, dropped what appeared to be a three-legged landing gear, and landed! The saucer was described as "metallic silver" in color and shaped like an inverted plate. It was captured on film by the two excited cameramen during its visit of several minutes.

Cooper phoned the Pentagon and asked what to do with the film. A general told him to have it developed and rush it to Washington, D.C. Since Cooper was not told he couldn't look at the film, he did so and verified the craft was "of unknown origin" and was as described by his camera team. (In those days test pilots knew of almost everything flying.) Cooper says the film was never seen nor heard of again, and could not be exhumed by researchers under the Freedom of Information Act.

Also in Chapter Four, Cooper revealed several pilot sightings with which he was familiar and which included a brief Roswell story. Here's the Roswell story:

A pilot and Air Force major, who was a good friend of Cooper's, was in Roswell at the time of the Roswell Crash. (One assumes that Cooper's friend was Major Marcel, who maintained until his death that the wreckage he examined was extraterrestrial, but Cooper does not name the man.) Cooper's friend told him the crash was "not a weather balloon," but was an aircraft of some kind and bodies were recovered. End of story.

During his astronaut years, Cooper became a good friend of Werner von Braun, the German rocket scientist then working for the United States. Cooper and von Braun spent hours together telling stories and sharing views on space exploration and the probability of life elsewhere in the universe. Naturally, von Braun had a UFO story for Cooper in exchange for the stories Cooper told.

On July 10, 1949, von Braun was working at White Sands Missile Range, New Mexico, when von Braun and

GROUNDED SAUCER ON TRIPOD

Photographed by Paul Villa, June 19, 1966 about 9:00 am, 3 miles west of Algondones and 30 miles north of Albuquerque, New Mexico. Remotely controlled discs seen by Mr. Villa were 3 ft. in diameter and 6 ft. in diameter. Photos courtesy Paul Villa and UFO International, Detroit, Michigan. Image shown similar to that described by astronaut Gordon Cooper and Bruce Henderson in *Leap of Faith*, sighting at Edwards Air Force Base, California, on May 3, 1957.

his team fired a V-2 and were tracking the rocket. The V-2 was traveling at 2,000 feet per second. Suddenly, the scientists saw "two small circular UFOs pacing the missile," von Braun told Cooper. One UFO was seen to pass through the V-2 exhaust, rejoin the other UFO, and speed away, leaving the missile far behind. The scientists were duly impressed with a technology which was years in advance of anything they knew about.

There is much more in this astronaut's revealing tale of flying and exploring the unknown. Not only is *Leap of Faith* a great story by an American hero, it is the witness of a strong advocate for the truth of UFOs and for an end to government secrecy about the subject. We in the UFO community are fortunate to have Cooper's voice added to this international investigation.

Chapter 14

Marine Pilot Reports UFO Over China Sea

My friend in Taos, New Mexico, served two tours of duty in Vietnam. A Marine Corps pilot, Carl was shot down twice. The second time, he served two and a half months in a Vietnam prison before repatriation. I have waited almost eight years to relate this pilot's UFO story, and now may do so, but only by using a pseudonym.

Carl and three other pilots were ordered to pick up four F8 aircraft in Hawaii in November 1965. Carl's aircraft was an F8U (Crusader), a single-seat jet fighter.

The four aircraft flew in formation to Guam, refueling twice in mid air. From Guam, they flew together toward the South China Sea, to rejoin their carrier, the *USS Coral Sea*. Carl, a brand new second lieutenant, flew in the No. 2 position. The flight flew west from Guam at 30,000 feet at 400 mph.

All of a sudden, on the intercom: "*Jesus,* what's *this?*" Carl looks to his right and sees a bell-shaped flying machine 600 to 800 feet away, just off the wingtip of the pilot in No. 4 position.

"*Jesus Christ,*" from another pilot. Carl looks again over his right shoulder, and sees the craft clearly. It was bell-shaped, and about the diameter of the wingspan, tip to tip, a distance of about 60 feet, Carl explained.

The pilots learned by radio that Guam had the intruder on their radar. After a few minutes, the strange craft raced ahead of the flight, rose, became a speck, and disappeared. No photographs of the strange craft were taken by the pilots.

After landing on the Coral Sea, the four pilots were told by flight commanders not to talk about their sighting. Soon they were debriefed by two officers from Naval Intelligence, and a second time by two Air Force Intelligence officers, who landed on the carrier by helicopter. A report was collected from each pilot.

Two of the pilots in this account did not return from Vietnam. The lead pilot, a 1st lieutenant at the time, is retired and living in Corpus Christi. Carl is trying to contact him for his input.

There is a footnote to this story. Carl said in his lifetime he has experienced four or five moments which were truly spiritual. This sighting was one of them. It caused him to think about how small a part of the whole we really are, how vast the universe must be, and it caused him to keep an open mind about strange things in the air.

"I know for a fact," Carl said, "that the ship we saw was not of this world."

Chapter 15

Budd Hopkins' Memoir

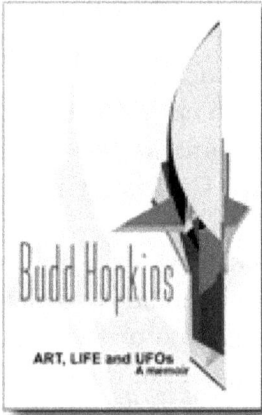

Budd Hopkins: Art, Life and UFOs, A Memoir
Budd Hopkins, Annalist Books, San Antonio (2009), with a few references from *Missing Time* (Hopkins, 1981)

Almost everyone in the UFO field has heard of Budd Hopkins, the abduction researcher, conference speaker, author of five books, numerous articles and interviews. Hopkins' fifth book, an autobiography, reveals a thoughtful, educated man who has led an extraordinary life and is willing to share it with readers.

At first, Hopkins was skeptical about UFOs and abductions. This mindset changed, however, after he and two friends experienced a close daylight sighting of a "roundish metallic thing" in 1964 over Cape Cod. Hopkins began reading about UFOs, keeping an open mind, and talking with friends about the subject.

In 1975, almost by accident, he stumbled upon his first UFO case. Known as the North Hudson Valley Landing, the case involves a close sighting of a UFO and occupants by a wine seller friend of Hopkins.

The wine seller friend, a "teetotaler," left his shop late one evening, homeward bound to New Jersey. A craft flew low over his car and hovered above the ground in a field next to the highway. The craft appeared to be 30 feet in length. A panel opened, a "ladder" was extended, and nine or 10 small figures descended ... "they looked like kids in snow suits," the wine seller commented.

The small "kids" dug holes for a time, while the wine seller watched from 60 feet away. Then they rejoined their ship and flew off.

In Hopkins' investigation ten months after the event, landing traces were found and corroborating witnesses were located. Hopkins found a family that, as a group, had gone outside their home to witness the low flying craft pass over their home.

At least two other eyewitnesses saw something strange, and a large plate glass window was shattered in a nearby apartment building, apparently after the craft took off.

I should mention that Hopkins is an abstract painter/ sculptor from New York City and is well known. His life story includes polio, his struggle to become a successful artist, his marriages, his many friends and some of his detailed UFO research efforts.

In his early days of UFO research, Hopkins connected with Ted Bloecher, the MUFON state director for New York and a person who was to become an invaluable aide to Hopkins as a research associate and consultant.

Bloecher connected Hopkins to a young fellow named Stephen Kilburn, who believed something strange and upsetting happened to himself, but he didn't know what. Recognizing a sincerity about the young man, Hopkins connected Kilburn with two psychologists— Drs. Franklin and Clamar—and a neurosurgeon by the name of Paul Cooper.

Hopkins hoped hypnosis could help the troubled youth as it had helped Betty and Barney Hill understand their trauma in *Interrupted Journey.* Under hypnosis, Kilburn related how his car on a lonely highway was "jerked" to the side of the road as if by a "magnet." He found himself surrounded by several "big-eyed" beings wearing "hooded one-piece suits," faces and hands "whitish," fingers smooth like "putty." Kilburn was encouraged to climb a ramp, enter a "saucer," and get on a table where he was examined. Dr. Cooper commented that he found the medical "spellbinding." The full story and tapes are related by Hopkins in *Missing Time* (1981) and abstracted in his memoir.

From the Kilburn tapes, Hopkins realized that hypnosis could be a valuable tool to unlock blocked memories in persons who believed they may have had alien contact or were suffering from psychic trauma of unknown origin. The artist apprenticed under eight or nine medical hypnotists over seven years before conducting his own medical regressions. His success with these cases—and some failures—are fascinating to read and ponder.

The author/artist includes in his memoir conversations and interactions with some of the most controversial men and women in the UFO field—Whitley Strieber, Carl Sagan, J. Allen Hynek, Shirley MacLaine and John Mack among others. Mack dedicated his book *Abduction* to "Budd Hopkins, who led the way."

After a careful reading of this smoothly written and gutsy study of the UFO field, it is clear Hopkins continues to lead, probe the alien mind, and inform the public.

Budd Hopkins passed on August 21, 2011.

Chapter 16

An Air Force Sighting Over the Lone Star State

An Air Force colonel came to Taos recently and related the following story to me.

When he was a young lieutenant, he and his instructor pilot were flying a T-38 aircraft over South Texas in September 1971. The T-38 is a hot Air Force jet trainer and has a ceiling altitude in excess of 40,000 feet. Just after sunset, both pilot and instructor sighted a strange object in the sky a little above their cruising altitude, which at the time was 37,000 feet. The object appeared round and dark in color. The pilot called Houston Radio and asked if they had the object on their radar scopes. They did not.

At this point the pilot and his instructor decided to have a closer look. It was a clear night, the colonel said, as he approached the stationary object from underneath at a speed of mach .94. At a distance of about a quarter-mile, he said the object appeared to be about the size of a football field. It had a domed top and appeared to be metallic. They could see red and green lights spaced evenly around the bottom rim of the craft. The colonel said they circled the large round object and kept it in sight for almost five minutes, then they watched as it departed at great speed.

Upon landing at their base, the young lieutenant and his instructor filed UFO sighting reports, each pilot being taken to a separate room to make his report.

Was the report classified? I asked. Perhaps it was at one time, but the colonel said I was free to write about it now. He drew a sketch for me to submit with my report of the event. Since the colonel is still on active duty, I have withheld his name from my account at this time.

Sketch drawn in 1997 by an Air Force colonel who saw this object at 38,000 feet over south Texas in September 1971

Chapter 17

Roswell: Fifty Years Later

My wife and I have another Los Alamos story to relate. By doing craft fairs for years in Los Alamos, my wife, Bella, has made a good friend there who is a librarian. I asked our librarian friend where the Lab library is because I wanted to go there and do some research. (The Lab library is different from the town library.)

"What kind of research?" she asked.

"Roswell," I replied. "I want to see what they have on UFOs."

Right away she said, "You're too late."

"Why is that?" I said.

"Because," said our friend, "right after 9/11 two men from Washington, D.C., came to the Lab, showed their ID, asked to go through everything they had on Roswell and UFOs. They looked at everything and took several publications away."

End of story. I still haven't gone through those Lab collections, but doing so is on my bucket list.

Southwest artist's weavings contain mysterious UFOs

by **Bella Sue Martin**

This photo has ships that show up on my weavings. I don't know how to weave circles or these discs and couldn't do it if I tried! I never plan or design them. They form themselves, and they just seem to occur randomly.

It is a truly exciting experience to be weaving and not know when they will show up. It is so magical to be weaving and then see these forms mysteriously grow in front of me. It has given my weaving another level of excitement. I used to be tired of threading my looms after 20 years. Now I can't wait to thread the loom as I know—or hope—that the ships again will appear.

I have had so many UFO experiences in Santa Fe and Taos that I know somehow these designs are coming from somewhere in a different dimension. What are they trying to tell me?

My weaving started out in a *very* mysterious way. I was in London at a Native American show at the Hayward Museum, called "Sacred Circles." I was a junior in college and just starting to weave. When I walked around at the show, I kept being drawn to this huge totem pole with an eagle on top. It was from the Northwest West Coast. I kept hearing a voice coming out from the totem pole, whispering, "Your path is now to be a weaver."

94

I then went out to the shops in London and stockpiled beautiful yarns. When I got back to the states, I changed my archaeology major to an art major and focused on weaving. That was in 1976.

When I moved to Austin, Texas, five years later, I went to a psychic—a very good psychic indeed—who read my palm and said, "There is a totem pole on your palm with an eagle on the top of it. In your past life you were a master totem pole carver in the Northwest Coast."

It wasn't until the next day that I remembered the London experience. This psychic knew nothing of my London trip and "Sacred Circles" experience. I got chills and then knew I was on the right path.

After moving to Taos, the Smithsonian saw my work in a gallery and invited me to send slides of my work for a show at the museum. I was one of 24 artists selected for this three-month show at the Smithsonian—the only weaver invited.

Now, UFOs are appearing in my weavings, and I feel rather enlightened and excited. They are trying to tell me something and I am looking forward to this new path of weaving. I am opening my own gallery in Taos in August, called "The Sacred Circle." Here I will show my UFO clothing pieces plus other artists of top-notch quality that I have met over the past 20 years by doing craft shows. Incredible transcendental glass jewelry and high-end clothing and jewelry. It is also my studio.

I'm not selling any of my UFO garments. I want to keep a record of what is happening. This morning (June 24, 1996) I had quite an elaborate form of mother ships with 12 smaller ships above it. So they are increasing in number!

Bella donated her framed weaving to the Roswell UFO Museum in 1997.

Chapter 18

Dan Aykroyd, Unplugged on UFOs

by **David Sereda**

A new film, *Dan Aykroyd, Unplugged on UFOs*, was released in May 2006. Nearly 50 years since an alleged UFO was sighted at Roswell, New Mexico, a new CNN/Time poll released recently shows that 80 percent of Americans think the government is hiding knowledge of the existence of extraterrestrial life forms. That is, nearly 230 million Americans are believers.

Many top grossing Hollywood films use UFOs, and ETs, but Dan Aykroyd is the first celebrity ever to apply brains and wit to disclose the real UFO phenomenon to the world in his new film, *Dan Aykroyd, Unplugged on UFOs*. Aykroyd proclaims, "Let's get past the debate on whether they are here or not. Let's start to analyze who they are, what their intentions are and how we can utilize this technology to better ourselves as a species."

Make no mistake about it, Steven Spielberg's UFO Blockbuster, *Close Encounters of the Third Kind*, was a box office smash hit in 1977, grossing $337,700,000 worldwide in 1977 dollars. At the American Institute for Economic Research, adjusted with inflation calculations, you get $1,106,162,541 in 2006 dollars.

Spielberg's *ET* grossed $792,910,554 worldwide in 1982; adjusted to 2006 dollars, we get $1,604,719,494.

These two UFO titles rival any movie made today. *ET* is still the top grossing film of all time.

What does that tell us? People want to know who is out there. Spielberg's *War of the Worlds* did $591,377,056 in 2005 dollars. Other titles like *Independence Day* ($816,969,255), *Men in Black, Star Wars,* and many more have spaceship or UFO implications. UFO titles rule at the box office for Hollywood, so why hasn't Hollywood gone deeper into the ET subject? Why haven't they sponsored deeper research into the phenomenon and given grants to many of the top researchers in the field?

Stephen Bassett, a UFO lobbyist in Washington, says most of the people in this field are broke and living in closets to do research. There is indeed a phenomenon happening in our skies, and because people want to know the answer, they conduct studies with pennies. So what would happen if a study was sponsored with millions of research dollars?

Dan Aykroyd is a self-sponsored researcher and has been since he was first aware of the UFO wave as a child. He learned about Kenneth Arnold's sighting in Yakima, Washington, in 1947, and he learned about the Roswell Incident. But Aykroyd doesn't stop there. It is his personal hobby to know the truth about UFOs. Now he does. He says "There is no debate anymore. UFOs are real. They are intelligently manufactured and guided technology from somewhere else, not this planet."

In this film, Aykroyd is backed up by many credible military personnel. NASA, Air Force and Astronaut (Gordon Cooper) told of his personal sightings of UFOs. Paul Hellyer, former Defense Minister of Canada, who at 82, went public at the University of Toronto in 2005 to say, "UFOs are as real as the airplanes that fly over your head ... That is my unequivocal conclusion."

Many top military witnesses have come forward to testify before their deaths, such as NASA astronaut Gordon Cooper, Colonel Phillip Corso, Paul Hellyer, Minister of Defense Canada, President Reagan, and more.

"It is the responsibility of scientists never to suppress knowledge, no matter how awkward that knowledge is, no matter how much it may bother those in power. We are not smart enough to decide which pieces of knowledge are permissible and which are not."

— Carl Sagan, in a 1991 commencement address at UCLA

Decide for yourself as you follow Dan Aykroyd through history and evidence, video footage and photographs and military eyewitness testimony. To see the trailer and more info, go to *www.DAUFO.com*.

The truth is finally disclosed.

Dan Aykroyd on UFOs

The following was found on the Web site http://ufonasa.terra-ent.com and includes a radio clip of Dan Akroyd.

In September of 1986, my wife Donna and I were in residence at our home in Chilmark, Massachusetts, on the island of Martha's Vineyard. On this particular occasion, there were two houseguests staying with us overnight. At about 2:00 a.m. I arose and stepped outside our bedroom onto the terrace wall to relieve my bladder. The firmament was magnificent, and it was natural for me to look up and observe its beauty and vastness.

After a minute or so, this contemplation was

interrupted by movement at the far right in my field of vision. At an altitude, which I estimated at around 100,000 feet (previous personal observations of the Concord making its turn towards Europe over the island at half that height substantiate my estimate), were two brightly glowing white dots traveling in tandem at high velocity. My immediate shouting awoke Donna, who came out to join me. She, in turn, recognized the mysterious glowing objects, and we both vocally aroused the couple who were asleep in the guest bedroom.

Drawn by the urgent and excited tenor of our voices, they too emerged and observed these two objects track across the night sky. It took less than a minute for the tiny, perfectly round, luminous bodies to traverse from right to left across the entire celestial array which was visible to us. The speed was evidently quite high.

We four agreed, through the filters of our pooled experience, that these could not be astral bodies, meteorites, planets, shooting stars, fighter jets, helicopters, airliners, or satellites. To me this was not some stirring revelation, for I have been intrigued since childhood by the possibility of such phenomena's existence. My sighting was a confirmation.

Like 50 percent of the North American populace (according to a Harris Upham poll), I have long believed in the reality of technically advanced craft with capabilities in speed and maneuverability far beyond any achieved by our aerospace manufacturers to date.

Roswell, Kecksburg, the last words of Captain Mantell, the account of Nebraska highway patrolman Herb Schirmer, the stories of Barney and Betty Hill, Travis Walton, Linda Cortile, and the Pascagoula and Alagash incidents are well known to me and to millions of people.

When this subject is discussed in my presence, people often say to me, "Dan, these are anecdotes! Where are the pictures, film, and videotape evidence?"

In fact, there are hundreds of thousands of such anecdotes (see the Laurence Rockefeller-funded report), thousands of hours of professional and home video (the Japanese Nippon TV footage of Area 51), and film dating from as early as the 1950s.

Dr. Roger Leir has made his life work the extraction and analysis of implanted objects from people who share the abduction experiences which have been catalogued by Budd Hopkins and Dr. John Mack.

In my view, and in that of millions like me, there is no question as to the existence in multiple of these advanced machines and in diverse forms—discs, crosses, wedges, triangles, boomerangs, cigars, and their respective occupants in various manifestations—Grays, Blues, humanoids, reptilians, and Mothmen, etc.

The question is not whether they exist but rather are some of them here to do our species harm or good?

Dan Aykroyd
C.M., D. Lit. (H.C.)

Chapter 19

Childhood's End Revisited
A UFO Memoir

"The old will become young again and the young will stay young."   — *George Van Tassel*

Here is a quiz which I have popped on my friends from time to time:

What do the books *Childhood's End, 2001: A Space Odyssey, The Martian Chronicles* and *Stranger in a Strange Land* have in common? If you said they are or were bestsellers, and they are all works of science fiction, you would be right on both counts.

A second list of book titles less well known, but having much in common with the first might read as follows: *When Stars Look Down, URI, The White Sands Incident, The Interrupted Journey, Behind the Flying Saucers, The Roswell Incident, The Day After Roswell.* These books on the second list all deal in various ways with extraterrestrials and other worlds, too, only they differ in one important respect from the books on the first list: the books on this second list and hundreds of others which might be included, are non-fiction. They are all saying flying saucers and space people are real! Pay attention!

My excursions into the UFO field began at Giant

Rock, California, in the 1970s. There, George Van Tassel, one of the leading contactees of the day, gave channelings in the Great Kiva and built his machine which he called the Integretron. I have already written about Van Tassel in Chapter One (p. 18), but I'm relating it now in more detail.

Rumea, my child friend, and I had gone to Giant Rock with some friends to find a man named Sami Sunsong and join his Majik Cirkus. A few miles from Giant Rock we passed a round building with a dome roof which looked somewhat like an observatory. This curious structure had port holes and was surrounded by a high wire fence and one of our group knew that inside was George Van Tassel's machine, the Integretron.

The building, together with just a little knowledge of what was inside, would pique anyone's curiosity and it piqued ours. My friends and I decided to pay Mr. Van Tassel a visit. Perhaps he would tell us about his machine, we thought, or about his experiences.

It was a Sunday afternoon. Mr. Van Tassel was at dinner with his family. He graciously sent word that we could wait if we wished to see him. After an hour or so, he came over to the living room where we waited and introduced himself. He quickly surmised that although we were intelligent and well-meaning people, we didn't know beans about this UFO business, which he had spent a large part of his life exploring and explaining. Nevertheless, he began a long monologue—a history really—of the UFO field as it had developed in modern times.

He told us of Kenneth Arnold's now famous sighting of the nine flying discs near Mount Rainier, Washington, in 1947; he told of the origin of the term "flying saucers," based on Arnold's description, "like a saucer turned upside down"; he related how this incident marked the

Kenneth Arnold, whose June 24, 1947 daylight sighting over Mount Rainier, Wash., started media coverage of "flying saucers"

Peter Crawford photo

beginning of the modern era of UFO sightings; he told us of his background as an aeronautical engineer and test pilot for Howard Hughes; and he told us of his attempts to make contact with UFOs by sitting outdoors in meditation and how it came about that he did make contact.

In 1953 a craft "landed" above ground at his Giant Rock airport, he said. Two men came over to him where he slept on the desert floor. They engaged him in conversation. They showed him their craft, which was unlike anything seen or dreamed of by Van Tassel. "Do you want to help your people?" they said to him.

"Who could say no to such a question?" Van Tassel said, enjoying his story as much as we were. Then they gave him plans and specifications for a machine which would regenerate organs and bodies, or so they said.

My friend, who was a student of the work of Nikola Tesla, the electrical wizard, must not have heard this last comment because he came forward in his chair and said, "Is the machine to be a source of cheap energy, then?"

"No," Van Tassel said patiently, "it is basically an oversize armature turning in a magnetic field. People will line up and pass through the force field thus generated and be restored to health and long life. It is an electrostatic magnetic generator for research into regeneration of minds and bodies. The old will become young again and the young will stay young."

Van Tassel told us many things that afternoon. He told us of how his friends, Frank Scully, author of *Behind the Flying Saucers,* and Captain Edward Ruppelt, author of *Report on Unidentified Flying Objects*, were harassed by a government whose policy was opposed to the free flow of information about UFOs. He told us the story of a crashed saucer in New Mexico, which was allegedly recovered by government troops and squirreled away for study in a top secret warehouse at Wright-Patterson Air Force Base in Ohio. He told us of Air Force and FBI confiscation of photographs of UFOs from private citizens, and of the Air Force debunking program of the 1950s and '60s, how the Air Force was ordered by the Pentagon to explain UFOs only as conventional objects or conditions.

Government consultants then made up explanations, such as swamp gas and swarms of bees, for perfectly valid sightings made by the public. "The government is guilty of a 30-year cover-up," Van Tassel said. Then he talked of the *Condon Report* of 1968, the University of Colorado's "scientific" study which was to present the truth of UFOs, but which instead became a "white-wash and scientific disgrace."

Somewhere in the conversation he mentioned how he respected psychic Uri Geller for speaking out about his connection with UFOs. But so few people were willing to speak out that Van Tassel had become discouraged. He had for years published a pamphlet titled *The Proceedings,* which in part contained information he said he obtained from space contacts. Over the years Van Tassel and his publications had attracted a small following of true believers and supporters, but he was pessimistic about changing race consciousness, even with information from space.

"What works, then?" I asked. "Can human nature ever change?"

"The Golden Rule," Van Tassel said. He had proven it 100 times in 100 situations.

As Van Tassel appeared tired, Gini, a folk singer with an angelic voice, offered to sing for him. We went out on the porch, where Gini had left her guitar. She sang a beautiful English ballad and her lyrical voice wafted across the desert floor even as her long, golden hair flowed with the wind. Our host appeared to enjoy the ballad and he asked Gini to sing another.

Then it was time for us to leave. We had received far more than we asked for in calling unannounced on this kind family man who had for so long held the contactee torch and carried the message that flying saucers are real.

I relate this interview with Van Tassel because it is special to me. Van Tassel has since died, but he got me to take seriously this UFO business and I have never regretted doing so. I am a writer and I love stories—especially flying stories—and the UFO stories are some of the most amazing you will ever hear or read.

Like all stories, they can become embellished as the years go by. Take, for instance, the story about the recovery by government troops of the fallen saucer in New Mexico. There is a sequel to this story. It is said that a few days later a great memorial flight of UFOs took place in the skies over Aztec, New Mexico. According to the story, hundreds of saucer craft were observed by local residents to pass in formation in a farewell salute to their fallen comrades. You see, there were occupants (extraterrestrials) in that doomed craft. Years later I was to learn that there had been a second saucer crash near Aztec, New Mexico, and bodies were recovered.

Theodora Anderson, my Hopi medicine woman friend, and her husband Thurston heard the crash story from a security officer and colonel at Kirtland Air Force Base who told them 12 bodies were recovered and that one had remained alive. Whether Theodora had reference to the Roswell crash or the crash at Aztec, I never learned.

Many who read this account will not believe. They will think it impossible for so great a secret as a recovered space craft, complete with bodies, to remain top secret all these years. For these skeptics I ask only that they read the book *The Roswell Incident* with an open mind, and then read *The Day After Roswell*.

Read and learn how an extraterrestrial craft was struck by lightning or disabled in some manner and crashed west of Roswell, New Mexico. How pieces (and bodies) were recovered by government troops from Roswell Army Air Base and transported by air to Wright-Patterson Air Force Base in Ohio, and to a medical facility located elsewhere; how eyewitnesses were ordered to keep silent about the discovery; and how the recovered fragments and the bodies were studied by government scientists and secrets learned leaked to defense industries.

Barry Goldwater, an Air Force general as well as a United States senator, heard the story and asked to see the saucer craft. He was turned down by his friend and senior officer, General Curtis Lemay, who told him, "You can't see it and I can't see it."

According to *The Roswell Incident,* President Eisenhower viewed the bodies during his presidency in the early 1950s, but was apparently talked out of informing the public as to the truth of UFOs by his intelligence advisors.

Some months after my interview with George Van Tassel, I am standing in my art gallery at Taos, New Mexico. The phone rings. It's Sami calling from York, Pennsylvania.

"Have you forgotten? We planned to go together to the UFO conference at Giant Rock, California." Sami is flying in to Albuquerque the next day. Can I pick him up and drive him to the conference?

Of course I can. I'm Sami's apprentice and a member of the Majik Cirkus Company. (Although I had forgotten about the conference.)

Two days later, Sami, an Oregon friend named Denny Saxman, poet friend Dick Whipple of Santa Fe and I are in my station wagon headed west. We drive through miles and miles of glorious desert country—past purple asters, yellow-gold chamisa, forest green juniper and pinyon mesas, arroyos, buttes, yucca, Navajo and Kayenta sandstone under vast blue skies, and then we are at our destination—Giant Rock in the heart of the southern California desert.

There in a campground at Giant Rock, cars and campers are parked every which way. We register for the conference at a long table. This conference is to take place outdoors and the fall weather is perfect—warm days, cool nights. We set up our sleeping bags amongst some boulders not far from the Giant Kiva and then we circulate among the hundreds of guests.

Some of the leading contactees of the West were

to be at the conference. Contactees are the folks that have had face-to-face contacts or conversations with extraterrestrials, or who say they have had such contacts. Van Tassel was one. And ever since his first contact, he had developed the ability to go into trance and allow extraterrestrials to speak through him. He held monthly channelings in the Great Kiva and interested persons came to the gatherings and listened as he channeled voices from space.

The voices spoke in English with strange foreign accents. These channelings were recorded and Van Tassel and his family sold tapes of the conversations to true believers or to students like myself who were trying to learn. The voices that spoke through Van Tassel spoke on science, religion, worship, human affairs and occasionally made predictions or took credit for some unexplained happening such as the New York electrical blackout of 1965.

So Sami and I and our other friends wandered about the desert conference grounds, talking to people and asking questions. Sami kept saying, "This is wonderful, wonderful. Even if it isn't true, it's still wonderful." Sami, an apostle of New Age culture, was undecided about UFOs. He had not been present when Rumea and I visited Van Tassel and this subject was new to him.

My poet friend, Dick Whipple, kept asking for proof of what was said, and of course, never being satisfied or shown definitive proof. It's hard to prove that flying saucers exist. In those days if anyone could prove it, the *National Inquirer* would pay them $1 million.

After Van Tassel's opening remarks to the conference, I went up to pay my respects to him and to say that I was a reporter and UFO investigator now, in part due to our previous conversation.

"Be persistent," he told me, "and you will be successful."

Then, one by one, the other contactees began to speak and I paid close attention to what was said. The article I wrote for *The Reporter* newspaper in Santa Fe tells the story better than I can now from memory, so I have included it here. The article, datelined Jan. 19, 1978, Santa Fe, New Mexico (slightly edited), reads as follows:

As everyone knows, truth is stranger than fiction—and flying saucers just might be able to travel faster than the speed of light. This is just one of the many space concepts introduced at Giant Rock, California, last October during the first Southwestern Regional Unidentified Flying Object Convention to be held at that remote desert campground and airstrip in seven years.

Giant Rock is a shrine in the legend and lore of flying saucers because it was at that ancient Indian holy place that George Van Tassel, one of the convention hosts, had his first physical contact with beings from another planet.

Van Tassel related the experience at the conference. He was sleeping on the desert floor. A ship came down at night; it "landed" above the ground. A man approached Van Tassel and brought him to the ship. Van Tassel was asked if he wanted to help his people.

He was told to build a machine. He was given a formula and other instruction. After 7 ½ years of "bench" research, he began work on the machine which now, more than 20 years later, is known as the Integretron and is housed in a dome-like structure near Giant Rock. Van Tassel describes his creation as a time machine which will be able to rejuvenate thousands of people as they pass within its force field. Van Tassel said the Integretron was

90 percent complete.

Because he has been contacted face to face in a physical way, Van Tassel is known as a flying saucer contactee. (His space contacts came from the star Epsilon Bode, a double star which we see in the sky as Arcturus. He said that *they* are doing research and gathering information on us.)

Another contactee, Dan Fry, author of *White Sands Incident*, told of the efforts to discredit him after he told of his encounter with a flying saucer in 1952 at White Sands Proving Ground in New Mexico, where he worked on a rocket test program. Fry related that he encountered the saucer and examined it, that a door opened, and that a being communicated with him mentally and offered him a ride. He said he accepted a ride to New York and back, which happened in minutes. The full story is told in his book.

A man named Hal Wilcox said that a contact was made between him and an orbiting space station in 1961, and that afterwards, a space being named Zemclaw appeared at his door. Wilcox told of going on trips in space ships, of staying four days on one planet, returning only to learn that a mere 15 minutes earth time had elapsed.

Wilcox said he brought back objects which were tested by the Rand Corporation, that he was tested by various research organizations, and that he passed the tests. He was taken on trips around this country and to Japan, and was assigned to explore a hidden city in the Yucatan.

Wilcox said he has had a varied background as a schoolteacher, private investigator, actor and writer, and that his present job is with "Logan's Run," the TV program. He said he doesn't try to prove his story to anyone anymore. He is learning to develop his abilities, he said, and he prefers to be a student.

There was a question-and-answer period after each speaker, and some of the questions asked Wilcox were: *What form of government do they have?* Answer: A counsel of governors. *What types of housing?* Answer: Domes and pyramid shapes, because these encourage life forces. One lady asked, "Do they have a god?" "We all have one God," Wilcox answered. "Let's just leave it at that."

Brian Scott's story is perhaps the strangest of all. In 1971, while hunting rabbits with a friend in the Arizona desert, he heard a noise, saw an object in the sky, was lifted along with his friend into the object. Later, under hypnosis, he and his friend related how they had received separate physical examinations, then were returned to the ground. Scott said that two years later it happened again, only this time he was given a tour of the spacecraft and was asked to step into a mind probe machine.

The space beings told him they could pick up anyone they wanted out of a million people, and they explained to him the meaning of a tattoo on his arm which had been there since he was 16 years old (1959). Scott was told to go to Tiahuanaco, Bolivia, and stand above a giant spider that looked like the image on his arm.

At first he refused to go, but a large orange fireball kept appearing in his home, and members of his family were injured by it and had to be hospitalized. Under hypnosis again (10 hours, videotaped at Anaheim hospital), 12 voices spoke through Scott. His doctors were told to be good to him because, in time, brilliant scientists would beat a path to his door. The doctors were also told that they didn't know very much about medicine. Scott was again told to go to a certain place in South America.

On December 22, 1976, Scott said he went to South America, found the spider, climbed up on a rock, spoke the code words given him by the space people, and underwent a "transformation." He became Voltar, the space being and former Inca priest and leader who had incredible powers, knowledge of photon, nuclear and solar power, pyramids and other secrets of the planet and or prehistory of the Inca people.

Some friends and a psychic researcher went with Scott to Tiahuanaco and filmed this transformation; it is reputed to be an amazing film, although it was not shown at the conference.

"I have seen so much, experienced so much, it is hard to relate to a general audience," he said at the conference. "Tell the people, show them," he said. "What the government won't tell us, we must find out for ourselves."

The guests at the conference were as interesting as the speakers. A woman named Marge told my friends and me that she channels for a certain space captain named Hilarion. As we talked to Marge, she would drop into trance, Hilarion would speak through her, and we could ask him questions and receive answers. I jotted down one of his comments. He said, "Lucifer was captured. Armageddon ended May 8, 1977."

Another guest, a minister and medium, had received the information that the space people were aware of the conference and were considering putting in an appearance. This channeling was printed up and handed out at the registration desk.

My poet friend, Dick Whipple, was skeptical of all that had occurred at this point. He was always saying, "The trouble with you, Jim, is you believe all this. You've lost your critical faculty."

"How do you know it isn't true?" I shot back.

I hoped there would be a demonstration for Dick and for all the other skeptics. And there was one.

Giant Rock is 50 miles north of Palm Springs. The desert is beautiful there, silent, often filled with cloudless and starry nights—as on the first night of the convention. Some of us were on the ground in our sleeping bags when there occurred an incredible light show: huge flashes of light, like heat lightning, lit up a close-by mountain range. (Giant Rock is in the center of a range of hills and boulders.) It lasted for 45 minutes, and five of us got out of our sleeping bags and stood on boulders and watched it.

The next morning I awoke with Dick standing over me.

"I suppose you want me to believe that 'demonstration,'" he said. "Well, there's a Marine base nearby, and it was the Marines."

"Dick, do you know that for a fact?" I protested.

He didn't, but his mind was made up, and I couldn't change it, even when I pointed out that there had been no sound, not a peep during the light show, and sound always accompanies the firing of heavy guns. Later I got a chance to ask Gabriel Green, president of Amalgamated Flying Saucer Club, about the demonstration. He hadn't observed it, but he said it was a device the saucers had used before to make their presence known.

Through the conference, there was an emphasis on getting along with one's neighbor, on giving and sharing information, on eternal man who lives forever, on people developing a more universal consciousness so that we humans can be brought into the federation of space brothers and sisters.

The conference was covered by a reporter or stringer for the *Los Angeles Times*. When I read his report in the *Times,* I realized he hadn't gotten the spirit of the conference at all, nor even the gist. If my error was in giving too much credence to what the contactees said, the *Times* reporter erred more seriously by not reporting what they said at all. This conference was about the contactees.

On the last evening of the conference, Brian Scott, one of the leading contactees, called a private meeting for contactees only. My friend Gini, the lady with the angelic voice, came and got me and brought me to the meeting. At the meeting, Scott asked all those who were contactees to raise their hands. Did they want to join the League of Contactees? Because if they did, they would then receive secret assignments which only they—as members of the League—could carry out. About ten people joined, as I recall. Not being a contactee, I didn't join. But I should have as I was a reporter, and ever since I have wondered about those secret instructions and the work of the league.

Later Gini asked me why I hadn't joined. "I'm not a contactee," I said.

"You are," she said. "You just don't know it yet."

Then Gini told me how she had seen a flying saucer in the California desert and her life was instantly changed by the observation. Gini said that immediately after she saw the spacecraft, she made a vow to use her greatest asset, her voice, not for money but only for the joy of giving.

We hugged and said goodbye and then Gini turned and added, "As long as you search for truth and beauty and do everything with love in your heart, you will be all right."

Good advice, I thought, even if hard to follow at times.

Chapter 20

Twinkle, Twinkle, Little Star

"We, too, are still far removed from perfection and have to evolve constantly, just like yourselves ..."
— *Semjase, Pleiadian cosmonaut,* Feb. 8, 1975
(*UFO ... Contact From The Pleiades,* Vol. I)

The following is based on *Messages From the Pleiades* (1988), *UFO ... Contact From The Pleiades,* Vol. I (1980) and Vol. II (1985), the video "Contact" (1988), *Light Years* (1987) and *Pleiadian Mission* (1994, revised 1998).

Twinkle, twinkle, little star; how I wonder what you are. Who among us has not looked up at the night sky and wondered? Are there planets whirling around those distant suns? Are there life forms?

As a child I often looked at the heavens and wished upon a star. Later, in university classes, I learned about our solar system and astronomy, but in those days questions about alien life forms were never asked.

As an Air Force navigator I was privileged to take altitude sightings on some of those luminous giants, and in the process Arcturus, Altair, Vega, Procyon, Polaris and Betelgeuse and I became acquainted. In the Air Force, too, I heard strange tales of unidentified flying

Jacobsburg-Allenberg,
Switzerland. Feb. 27,
1975, 16:00
Eduard Meier Variation II
(our designation)

(*Courtesy Wendelle
Stevens, Tucson,
Arizona*)

objects, but I was too busy working to pay much attention to them.

Only later, as I began to explore the UFO field in earnest, were my eyes opened to the possibility of extra-terrestrial visitations.

Space Science Center

I was fortunate to live in Santa Fe, New Mexico, where there was an unusual nonprofit facility called the Space Science Center. At the center, its creator and amicable director, C. de Baca, showed educational videos and films to school classes and the general public interested in astronomy, the training of astronauts, space travel, the mysteries of the Bermuda Triangle, and similar subjects. My astrologer friend, Theodora Anderson, and I were frequent visitors. Theodora was also head of our UFO study group. In the 1970s, she had learned the truth about the crash at Roswell, as I had learned it independently from a different source. Together we attempted to share the secret with others and the public. The secret that alien life beings were here was too great to be bottled up by the military, or so we believed, and I still believe.

On one occasion, when I stopped by the Space

Science Center, de Baca told me he had written NASA, asking them for anything on UFOs. By return mail he had received some interesting film footage and asked if I would care to have a look. Of course, he knew I would.

A few moments later, we were seated in the darkened theater, the film rolling. As related in Chapter One (p. 17), the raw footage showed an astronaut at a window of a space shuttle. He was filming an object or objects with a hand-held video camera. As the film unrolled, we observed two objects flying a course parallel to that of the shuttle. The objects were glowing and oval in shape and not unlike the objects I had observed at close range in the Bermuda Triangle a few years before (related on p. 21). *Hello again,* I said, smiling.

The next day de Baca was ordered by NASA to return the footage. When he delayed, the FBI paid him a visit to retrieve the film. "The long-standing policy of cover-up continues," I commented. Then I recalled the words of one of the contactees: "What the government won't tell us we must find out for ourselves."

Pima Air Museum

In my work as an art dealer, I travel the West a fair amount. One day, while traveling through Arizona, I get nostalgic for my old aircraft, the C-124 Globemaster, and my shipmates of long ago. I remember there is an air-craft graveyard near Tucson, so I motor over to it. At the airpark they tell me they don't have the C-124. I go in, anyway, wandering among the aircraft, recalling dawn take-offs, long flights of incredible beauty and danger and strenuous Arctic adventures.

Suddenly I see it—the 124! After 3,000 hours of crew time in that flying machine, I would know its shape any-where. After I pay my respects to her and say prayers for

Bachtelhornli, Switzerland, March 28, 1976, 16:00,
Eduard Meier, Variation III
(Courtesy Wendelle Stevens, Tucson, Arizona)

some fallen comrades, I return to the Air Museum office. That's where my eye falls on the book *UFO ... Contact From The Pleiades.* To say the least, the close-up photographs struck me like a beam of light. And the text and quotes addressed questions I had pondered for years.

I knew flying saucers were real. I knew the Roswell crash was real. These close-ups of space ships had the look and feel of the real thing, too! Then and there I bought the book and began my study of the Meier Chronicles.

The Meier Chronicles

Several books, hundreds of photographs and a video describe the Eduard "Billy" Meier contacts. Meier is on one level a simple Swiss farmer with less than a high school education, yet he is self-educated from extensive travel and was apparently tutored to an advanced level by several mentors.

According to Randolph Winters, author of *Pleiadian*

Mission, Meier was taught by extraterrestrials mentally and in ships since he was seven years old. Winters spent five months with Meier in 1989 and was privileged to discuss almost every aspect of the case with Meier.

In January 1975, Meier was permitted to take a series of extraordinary photographs of UFOs. These are believed by many of us to be photos of "beamships" from another solar system. The photographs taken by Meier are crystal clear and reveal metallic vehicles some seven meters (22.75 feet) in diameter, in various flying modes. Photos of the beamships are reproduced in several books and in the video *Contact*, which describes Meier's experiences.

Meier's photographs have been examined by scientists and photographic experts in Europe and the United States, and appear to be as represented, i.e., photos of UFOs from beyond Earth. A team of investigators headed by Wendelle Stevens of Tucson, Arizona, and including Lee and Brit Elders of Munds Park, Arizona,

Bachtelhornli, Switzerland, March 28, 1976, 16:00.
Eduard Meier
Courtesy Wendelle Stevens, Tucson, Arizona

has subjected the photos, along with recorded engine sounds, landing sites and a metal fragment, to extensive tests.

The case, however, has not been without detractors, including two leading UFO clubs in the United States. The claims for and against Meier are examined in detail in *Light Years*, as are related events such as the now discredited *"Condon"* report which attempts to put the "kiss of death" on legitimate UFO sightings by reliable witnesses. No field of study has ever had so many self-styled debunkers and paid disinformation agents as the UFO field.

However, it is not the purpose of this review to prove or disprove anything. What is more interesting to students of UFOs who know they exist is what alien visitors have come to tell us. This also is the thrust of Winters' book, *Pleiadian Mission*, and the other books reviewed here.

Who are these visitors and why have they come? What is the nature of their society and is it true that they have discovered how to fly faster than the speed of light? Have they come to harm us or to help us?

Meier is contacted telephathically prior to each face-to-face contact. As extraterrestrial woman by the name of Semjase (*Sehm-yah-see*) invites Meier to meet her at a remote rural location. When Meier reaches the contact site, usually by moped, Semjase in her silver beamship flies in. It sounds like a Gothic romance—this one-armed man and his lady from the galaxies—only it is so much more. For some it is a fraud. For the investigative team, it became an almost unsolvable mystery. For students of UFOs, like myself, it answered questions.

Over the years Meier interviewed Semjase many times. "There is no need to take notes," she tells Meier

Hinwil, Switzerland, February 1975
Eduard Meier and family shortly after the contacts with Semjase began
Courtesy Wendelle Stevens, Tucson, Arizona

in fluent German at the first meeting. Later she will transmit their conversation telepathically and he need only write it down.

Semjase's Planet

Semjase tells Meier she comes from the Pleiades, a star cluster many of us see in the night sky and called the Seven Sisters. Meier notes that Semjase looks like an attractive Earth woman in her mid-30s, although she says she is 330 years old. He relates that she has red hair and her eyes are shaped differently than are human eyes, but she does not allow him to take a photograph of her. It could compromise her Earth appearance, she said in *Message From the Pleiades* by Stevens.

Semjase says her home planet is called Erra. It is slightly smaller than Earth and revolves around the star Teygeta. It supports a population of 17 billion. Erra is governed by a one-world government and ruled by a high council which governs all the Pleiadian worlds. People live in single-family circular dwellings on a plot of ground where vegetables are cultivated.

"Each person contributes toward a sharing with all," Semjase told Meier. Family planning is mandated and married couples remain in that state for life. However, Winters writes in *Pleiadian Mission* that two or three marriages and families at the same time are common and that jealousy and envy are almost unknown. According to Semjase, communication on the home planet is by telepathy.

The Beamship

The Pleiades is located 500 light-years from Earth, only the journey takes a mere seven hours, according to Semjase. In 1981, she allowed Meier to photograph Variation VI Beamship, a new type which could make the leap from the Pleiades to Earth in a scant seven minutes.

Winters, in *Pleiadian Mission*, explains how this is possible. The beamship is converted into particles of matter which travel faster than light through something called "hyperspace." Semjase's mother ship, located in deep space, can also travel many times the speed of light.

Semjase says she is not permitted to give Meier details of the ship's flight mechanism except to say that they have learned how to manipulate time and can fly billions of miles in a fraction of a second. "Earth governments only want the flight drive information to dominate others and to attempt to rule the cosmos," Semjase tells Meier.

Semjase's beamship, one of six she appears in over the years of the Meier contacts, is often hidden from view by "deflector screens" to avoid being seen by the uninvited.

Berg-Romlikson, Switzerland, June 12, 1975, 10:40
Eduard Meier, Variation II (our designation)
Courtesy Wendelle Stevens, Tucson, Arizona

On one occasion, however, the beamship was intercepted by a Mirage jet from the Swiss Air Force. Photographs of the encounter are reproduced in two of the books. Apparently the jet lost in this encounter, as the investigative team unearthed reports that the jet returned to its Swiss base with damage to its fire control system.

"All beings have the right to defend themselves," Semjase told Meier after the incident occurred.

In 1976, a few of Meier's friends were permitted to view the alien spacecraft. Meier himself was beamed aboard and taken on a tour of the solar system and several nearby stars, he said. Even Winters, during his visit to see Meier, observed one of the Pleiadian ships.

Conversations Between Semjase and Meier

In her conversations with Meier, Semjase spoke of

the prehistory of Planet Earth, of how Earth people have common ancestry with her own race, of the date of the great flood and its cause by a comet, and of mysteries of the Bermuda Triangle. She also spoke of the Aquarian Age and how it will bring to Earth people "real life and allow everything to develop to its highest potential, including spirit."

In 1975 Semjase told Meier of the hole in the Earth's ozone layer over the South Pole. She asked him to write a letter to a Harvard University professor warning of the condition, and on February 25, 1975, a letter was sent but no reply was received.

Meier said he and Semjase held over 100 face-to-face meetings. They talked of Earth contactees and false contactees, of other alien societies visiting Earth, of astral travel and past lives, of hyperspace drive and of Earth religions which Semjase said often enslave men rather than reveal the truth. Semjase takes almost as dim a view of Earth religions as she does of Earth governments, for which she has absolutely no use. Her mission, she tells Meier, is to tell Earth people that they are not alone in

Bachtelhornli, Switzerland, March 28, 1976, Eduard Meier
Courtesy Wendelle Stevens, Tucson, Arizona

the universe; she also comes to teach the nature of life.

Semjase predicts public landings of extraterrestrials by the year 2000. These aliens will not come to harm us, she said, but rather are in the nature of our evolution, and they will not be from the Pleiades. Her race is too advanced for Earth development, she said.

Spiritual Values

On Meier's 10th contact with Semjase, she spoke of spiritual values.

"The human being is the carrier of the spirit, which never dies and which also in his deepest sleep does not sleep; which records all thoughts and movement; which tells the human being whether his very thoughts are right or wrong ... the spirit holds the outlook for perfection, harmony, peace, recognition, understanding, knowledge, wisdom, truth, beauty and love in all things ... He (man) himself is the heavenly kingdom, the domain of Creation ..."

Semjase reminds Meier that she and her race are not gods, and that her own race is "far from perfection and must evolve constantly."

Part of Semjase's mission is to teach about "The Creation," an ageless nonjudgmental, spiritual force, according to Semjase and Winters, and is "eternal knowledge which guides the growth of the universe." Winters says that Meier's last contact with Semjase was in 1984.

The Billy Meier contacts and related UFO materials open a whole new field of inquiry for those that have eyes to see and ears to hear. Whether the books are read as fact or fiction, they are full of fascinating, mind-expanding ideas for the scholar, scientist and student of cultural anthropology, like myself. The world is changing fast, and UFOs are an important element in that change.

Chapter 21

How to Become a Cosmic Citizen

"You have put things in a way people can understand—very accurate and tasteful. The hope is many will read and apply what is there—keep up the great work —you are a bridge between worlds—Namasté"

— 'Sara 5' to the author

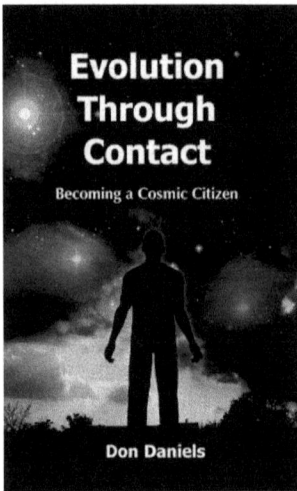

Evolution Through Contact
Becoming a Cosmic Citizen
Don Daniels

Evolution through Contact: Becoming a Cosmic Citizen
Don Daniels (2012)
978-1-470063-95-5, ETC Books
Evergreen, Colorado

Guest review by **Ann Ulrich Miller**

As a commercial airline pilot, Don Daniels steps bravely out of the mainstream into disclosure with his book, *Evolution through Contact,* in which he writes about his experiences with Dr. Steven Greer and CSETI (Center for the Study of Extraterrestrial Intelligence), initiated by his curiosity and desire to contact beings from beyond this world.

Unlike most pilots, who would choose to remain

silent about UFOs and ET contact, Daniels wants people to know that such contact is an important step in our society toward progressing not only as a species but in bringing forth important, suppressed technology and wisdom to benefit humankind. In his book he tells of his journey toward awareness and understanding, and inserts humor, inspirational tales and commentary, along with his own poetry. The book is well documented with footnotes and has an index in the back so the reader can do more exploring on their own.

If you've ever wanted to know what it's like to be in communication with ETs, or what occurred behind the scenes at the Disclosure Project that was presented at the National Press Club in May 2001, this book provides answers. Daniels took part in the 2001 Disclosure presentation in Washington, DC. His book also covers the misunderstood *Condon Report,* what you should do if you are "psychotronically" attacked, and how to prepare yourself for ET contact, among other subjects, such as out-of-body travel.

In his Preface, Daniels explains how the book started out as a simple "how-to" for preparing yourself for your own ET contact experiences. He wanted to suggest some ways to attempt initiation of contact. It soon developed into a treatise on becoming a Cosmic Citizen. Of course it is up to each individual whether they wish to personally ascend or else remain in the familiar fear-based world of separation and limited consciousness. Many continue to sleep, unaware of the epic decisions we face.

Daniels' book tells about many of his own personal experiences. He had an early interest in things that flew—which included paper airplanes, balsa wood gliders, rubber-band powered planes, kites, model airplanes and radio-controlled airplanes. He writes:

"My first thoughts that I remember about UFOs and Extraterrestrials were in the 6th grade. I had a rather boring teacher, and when I wasn't challenging her on some point of scientific fact, the environment tended to foster my tendency to daydream. One of my common daydreams was of a flying saucer landing on the schoolyard, and my going out to meet the occupants. I thought that would be very cool, and I don't recall ever having any fear about such an encounter.

"I don't know what prompted this daydream other than having a father who was rather open-minded and discussed such issues and possibilities as UFOs with us. I suppose it is possible that I had some earlier contact, either on a physical or telepathic level, but to this date I have no conscious memory of such."

He tells about how, in junior high, he started flying "real airplanes," taking some formal lessons in his father's Cessna 206 when he was 14. "This was so that I would be a more fully qualified co-pilot on family trips and be able to land the plane myself if the need ever arose. I knew from even that time that I wanted to be a professional pilot, and my life and education were centered upon that goal."

On his 16th birthday (the youngest you can solo a powered plane), Daniels got up early, rode his bicycle to the airport, and went flying with his instructor. The weather cooperated, and on February 26, 1968 the instructor got out and he took flight alone for the first time.

As his aviation progressed, Daniels grew aware through some of his friends that exploration of the paranormal—either UFOs or mystical studies—would impede his aviation career progression. He writes, "While I still read the occasional book on the subject, I kind of put it all on the back burner for a while." He got a job as a flight instructor in Oakland, California. His new wife, Terry, "quickly got bored sitting around the apartment, so she signed up for the Aircraft Mechanics School at the College of Alameda. I was about to learn that whenever this gal took on a challenge like that, she went after it with uncommon passion."

Working out of the Oakland Airport for several years, the Danielses occasionally drove past the Rosicrucian Order buildings and their magnificent Egyptian Museum in San Jose, California. "We wondered what it was all about," writes Daniels, "but never stopped in. This was the time a number of cults were active in the area, and I just didn't know what was what. We didn't want to get sucked into some cult that sounded good at first, and then pulled you in deeper and deeper. Besides, it would not mix well with my professional career. Again, I put mystical inquiry on the back burner due to career and peer pressures, but I still had this strange longing for answers that never went away."

It was years later, when he made the mystic connection. Daniels was working as a Boeing 727 flight engineer in San Francisco. "During the first year I flew a few times with a really outside-the-box captain," he explains. "This guy was a real free spirit with a subtle wry sense of humor. He would shovel all kinds of crazy stuff at me, and I would just heap it right back at him. We got along famously, much to the bewilderment of the co-pilots.

"One day, while flying between Yellowstone and Jackson Hole, he dared me to explain to the passengers how the Grand Tetons got their name. ... I declined, since I was still on probation, and instead handed him the PA. He chickened out and gave the passengers the straight spiel instead, 'Off to our left you can see Yellowstone Lake, and off to the right Jackson Lake and the Grand Tetons.' If you have ever seen the movie *Space Invaders,* Captain Jack had to have been the character study for the Martian pilot *Blaznee.* He had that kind of personality.

"On one layover the whole crew went across the street to dinner at a place called Gaylin's Ribs, and one of the flight attendants asked Jack about his ring. He said that it was a Rosicrucian Ring. My radar went right up, and as soon as I could get him alone, I was pumping him for information about the Rosicrucian Order.

"Well, this sounded like what I had been searching for so long, and my interest was renewed. Later that month we had a Spokane layover, so we planned for my wife to meet us all for dinner. Jack brought along his girlfriend (now wife) and we talked about the Rosicrucian Order all evening. To make a long story short, Terry and I wound up joining and it has been a fascinating mystical study ever since."

Why is the Rosicrucian Order important to the UFO story? Daniels explains that, among other things, they taught him to be open-minded and to consider a multitude of different viewpoints on subjects that sometimes go against popular opinion. He writes, "I also came full circle in another way. Since I was flying out of San Francisco, I often visited the Rosicrucian Park and the magnificent Egyptian Museum in San Jose that I had looked at from the outside and been drawn to all those years before."

He was also reviving his interest in UFOs and even wanted to get involved in UFO/ET investigation and research. There was an awful lot of disinformation and just plain confusion going on in the field, so he wanted to find out who was reputable.

"One of the Rosicrucian members was also a member

of MUFON (Mutual UFO Network)," he writes, "and he gave me some literature, but it just didn't feel quite right to me at the time, so I kept looking.

"Several years later, after we had moved to Colorado, my wife noticed that a Dr. Steven Greer was going to be speaking on UFOs in my town the following week. I checked my schedule and found I could just make it if I got back from my trip on time. Bone tired from several days on the road, I dragged myself down to the evening lecture and in just an hour or so Dr. Greer tied together almost all the loose ends that I had been trying to put together for so many years."

Daniels says that everything just suddenly fit, the "why" became obvious, and he knew that this Dr. Greer was onto something. "Right away I started making plans to attend the CSETI Ambassadors to the Universe training that summer. I didn't know how I was going to do it as I had no summer vacation that year, but I finally just made the commitment, sent in my application, and trusted it would work out."

Daniels had his first UFO sighting on that CSETI outing with Steven Greer in 1999, which he relates early in the book and discusses in more detail in his "Paradigm Shift" chapter. He tells of the remote viewing that took place, and how this experience changed his life.

One of the most fascinating chapters in Daniels' book talks about his encounter with Tashina (or "Sara 5"), an ET among us. She claims to be "from an unnamed 5th Dimensional world," he writes, "and now says she is Arcturian." He originally gave her the pseudonym "Sarah 5" due to her similarity to the heroine in Mark Kimmel's *Trillion* trilogy. "She has since asked that I use her spiritual name Tashina in the book instead," he explains. This woman and other intriguing acquaintances he meets in the flesh are spine-tingling and inspirational confirmation that ETs are among us.

This book relates many of the author's personal experiences, but the journey is really more about the reader. There are many suggestions and concepts offered that should help you move towards Cosmic Citizenship. After reading the book, you will feel transformed.

Chapter 22

Contact from Sirius-B

"There is only one consciousness. One light shines through the human being and the light is divine. Everything in this universe has its appropriate place. Every event has its appropriate hour."

— Frank

Permutation, A True UFO Story
Shirlè Klein-Carsh and
Ann Carol Ulrich (1993)
Earth Star Publications
Pagosa Springs, Colorado

Guest review by **Ann Ulrich Miller**

It was in the summer of 1988 that I met Shirlè Klein-Carsh, an artist and an associate director of UFO Contact Center International. We met in Laramie, Wyoming, at the Rocky Mountain Conference on UFO Investigation, which was put on each year by Dr. R. Leo Sprinkle, professor emeritus. Shirlè had come from British Columbia and was staying with the UFO Contact

Center's founder, Aileen Edwards (now Aileen Garoutté). I was so taken by Shirlè's story that I offered to help her write a book about her experiences.

In early November 1988, Shirlè took me up on my offer and flew into Grand Junction, Colorado to spend several days with me and my family in nearby Delta. We interviewed intensely for the book, which was a work in progress for several years. It was finally published in 1993 under the title *Permutation, A True UFO Story*. Even though I did the work of organizing and actually writing the book, it is totally Shirlè's story. She dictated on tape and I transcribed and edited as needed. She provided a multitude of original art work from her cosmic and futuristic paintings.

Shirlè Klein-Carsh in Laramie, Wyoming, 1988

In 2013 her book has been republished in a slightly revised form. The first edition sold out within the first couple of years and it was only in 2012 that I convinced her to let me revise and reprint *Permutation*.

Shirlè was born in Montreal and has lived in Canada her whole life, except for a few months in Australia (an important time which is covered in her book). Her father, her mother, two sisters and a brother lived with her in a typical Jewish surrounding. She tells the story of how her mother, Bella Edelstein, was visited by an angel on the day Shirlè was born. Bella and her husband Meyer, Shirlè's father, had immigrated to Canada from Poland. While Bella lay suffering on her hospital bed, feeling scared and alone, and missing her homeland, an angel suddenly appeared

before her and offered Bella a glass of orange juice.
"The child you are carrying is very special, Bella. This child will someday be very famous and is indeed a special child," the angel told her mother. After Bella finished the orange juice, she felt instant relief and settled back, closing her eyes. When she looked again, the angel had disappeared but the empty orange juice glass was on the table beside her. Shirlè, whose birth name was actually Sarah, was born shortly afterwards.

There were several experiences Shirlè had as a child and as a young woman that indicate that she had a connection with space beings. Her life was unusual in the respect that she had a husband who was her soulmate—Hymie Klein—and he encouraged her to stray from the expected role of women in the 1950s to focus on becoming an artist instead of a housewife. Hymie wanted Shirlè to be able to fend for herself if the need should arise. And it did.

It was in 1971, three years after Hymie's untimely death, that Shirlè moved to Vancouver to be closer to her daughter and granddaughter. She was riding in a car with a mathematician friend down Fourth Avenue in Vancouver when—suddenly—Shirlè made him stop in front of a second-hand store. She wanted to go inside.

"*That* shop?" Her companion chuckled. "Look at it. You want to go inside *there?*" He obviously was not impressed.

But Shirlè insisted they go in. Reluctantly he followed her in. She didn't really notice the man inside the shop right away, but he was someone in his mid or late forties with long black hair and a sallow or light brown complexion. She wandered around the shop, wondering what she was doing there. Meanwhile, the mathematician friend walked over to the man and saw that he was working on some equations.

"Oh ... my ... what is it you're doing there?" asked her friend. "What are all these equations?"

The man in the shop turned to him and said, "It's not of this world."

Right away, when Shirlè overheard that remark, she slapped her cheek and thought, *Dear God, a nut!*

Just as she reacted, she noticed the man turn to stare at her. He had huge, saucer-shaped eyes that looked black from where she stood. He looked right at her and smiled, as if he had read her mind.

The mathematician friend tried to get some answers out of the man in the shop, but he had no luck. Finally, Shirlè settled on some doo-dad in the store and brought it up to the counter. In a cocky fashion she asked the man, "Well, when are they going to take me?" She was referring to an experience she'd had in college, when two people in "wet suit gear" had appeared at her bedside.

The man kept a straight face and told Shirlè, "I'll find out."

As they left the shop, her friend remarked that the math he had seen made his own knowledge look primitive. "What's going on here?" he ranted. "I feel like I don't know anything now."

Shirlè kept going back to the shop on Fourth Avenue and became acquainted with the man in the shop, whose name was Frank. Three or four times a week she would go and he was always there. It was the beginning of an ongoing two-year friendship in which Frank, who was Shirlè's space contact, taught her many things and informed her about things that would happen in her future.

Permutation, A True UFO Story is about Shirlè Klein-Carsh's evolvement and the many life challenges she had to go through to attain her spiritual level. The book contains some remarkable events and paranormal experiences. She was tested over and over again and proved that she had the integrity the space people required for her to be one of their "sub-agents." She eventually made it as an artist and she became involved in helping many others with their own space contact experiences, including her position as an associate director of UFO Contact Center International.

There are some fascinating passages in her hypnosis session and in transcriptions of several séances she sat in on with George Major of Sirius-B and beings by the name of Kromme and Middle C. Probably the most amazing part of Shirlè's life story is the fact that she bears proof of her contact with Frank. Before he left, he gave her eight copper plates which he engraved with symbols from his planet. She kept those plates and was gifted with an interpretation of them by a psychic friend.

Her story is one that deserves a place among the most well known contactees of our generation. She currently resides in the Vancouver area with her husband, Fred Carsh, and her surrealist paintings can be viewed on line at her Web site, *http://nsartists.ca/shirlekleincarsh.*

The book is available from CreateSpace.com or Amazon.com and is also in eBook form. You can order it through Earth Star Publications, at *www.earthstarpublications.com/Permutation.html.*

Ann Ulrich Miller is the publisher of *The Star Beacon,* the bi-monthly metaphysical newsletter from Earth Star Publications in Pagosa Springs, Colorado.

Chapter 23

We Are Not Alone

By **Mary Mageau**

The universe as we know it is expanding rapidly. Our sun is one of 100 billion stars in our galaxy with planets revolving around them. The Hubble space telescope has shown us that our Milky Way Galaxy is only one of possibly 200 billion galaxies. Only the universe knows how many possible planets have intelligent life on them. Space is not empty as even a vacuum contains tremendous amounts of background energy. The majority of the cosmos is dark matter—that is, for each particle in our tangible universe, there may be something like a trillion shadow particles in universes in other dimensions.

One of the great central mysteries of the creation states that hydrogen burns inside stars with an efficiency of 0.007 to produce helium. If hydrogen burned at 0.008, the hydrogen would have burned to helium by now, and our universe would consist of nothing but gas balloons. If it burned at an efficiency of 0.006, our universe would consist of nothing but hydrogen and only a little helium. Life, however, cannot exist in an environment containing only hydrogen or only helium as complexity is required: the heavy elements such as carbon, oxygen, phosphorus and so on. As these are cooked inside of stars, to achieve this possibility hydrogen must burn with the correct efficiency of 0.007, neither more nor less. Somehow the properties of hydrogen have been perfectly fine-tuned for building the heavy elements required for life. If gravity was even slightly stronger than it is, the stars would burn so fast there would be no time for life to evolve. If the universe expanded even slightly faster than it does, it would have dispersed before matter had a chance to collapse into stars and planets. If the perfect irregularities weren't planted within it, we would either be sucked into black holes or dispersed as a rarefied gas with no stars, no planets and no life.

Science is in general agreement about the existence of a Big Bang, from which our universe is said to have literally exploded into life. The problem science faces with this theory is the same difficulty that a Big Bang itself would face in successfully creating life. In his book *The Life of the Cosmos,* physicist Lee Smolin details the many variables which had to be exactly balanced in order for the universe to unfold into living order, rather than random chaos. The mass of the proton, the strength of gravity, the range of the weak nuclear force, and dozens of other variables determine how a universe will unfold after a Big Bang. If any of these values had been just slightly different, the universe would have become a disorganized pool of hot plasma, where galaxies and solar systems were unable to form.

And so it seems that the universe has been deliberately structured so as to be friendly to life. As some power or force has worked things in this way, that is to make life central to the whole cosmos, then the cosmos itself must also be a living entity. Theorists tell us that the cosmos is an integrated system that is deeply and totally unified in some mysterious way. Immense levels of energy flow constantly through the universe and continuously regenerate it. As physicist Brian Swimme describes it, "The universe emerges out of an all-nourishing abyss not only 15 billion years ago, but in every moment." Thus everything in the universe is a flowing movement that arises with everything else, moment by moment, in a process of continual regeneration.

The Disclosure Project

While contemplating the rich tapestry of potential life the universe harbors, how can we be so naïve as to think that our one tiny Earth planet might be the only place in the universe to contain living, evolving beings? Are we really alone in this vast universe? On May 9, 2001, one of the largest and most successful press conferences, known as The Disclosure Project, was completed. Under the direction of Dr. Steven Greer and held at Washington, DC's National Press Club, more than 20 military, government and corporate witnesses gave testimony before millions of people and the international media.

The witnesses spoke under oath about the vast cover-up of unambiguous UFO and extraterrestrial events over the past 50 years. Further information, books and video recordings are available from The Disclosure site at *http://www.disclosureproject.org*, and see also the Vatican's site acknowledging the existence of extraterrestrials at *http://www.ufodigest.com/balducci.html*

The ramifications of the proof that we are not alone in the universe moves far beyond the extraterrestrial presence. Many covert groups within all of the major world governments have initiated a total cover-up of their many interactions with extraterrestrial races. In addition, these covert governmental groups are withholding valuable technologies gained by the reverse engineering of UFO spacecraft. Their presently hidden knowledge of zero point, anti-gravity cold fusion energy would enable us to immediately remove our dependence on fossil fuels, thus halting the threat of global warming. Our ability to harness free zero-point energy technology would enable us to clean up our severely degraded planetary environment, to heat and light our homes and grow our food in non-polluting ways, without the need for either electric or nuclear power sources.

Of most urgent need, however, is a requirement, confirmed in legislation, binding world governments to ban all weapons from space and to cease targeting peaceful extraterrestrial vehicles (UFOs). We share all of multi-dimensional space with many other galactic civilizations far in advance of ourselves, both spiritually and technologically. It is their desire to welcome Planet Earth and her inhabitants into the interplanetary community, but this will only be attained when humanity is able to achieve peaceful negotiations and resolution of its conflicts, both globally and in space.

In order to maintain the momentum of The Disclosure Project information, we must speak out and contact members of governments and the United Nations to request and support honest open hearings on the following: the UFO issue, the total ban on the weaponizing of space and the declassification of advanced energy and propulsion systems connected to UFOs and extraterrestrial objects. The time has come to tell the world that we are not alone and that the solutions for many of humanity's problems are held in secret classified projects that require immediate disclosure.

Beyond the limited perceptions of our third dimension, there is a multitude of highly evolved and fully conscious beings, both spiritually and scientifically far in advance of ourselves, who are known collectively as the Galactic Federation of Light. The Federation represents many different races, some in humanoid form like ourselves, and others not. Their diversity of appearance is the result of the unique planetary environments (atmosphere, temperature and gravity) in which the various races emerged and developed.

The first on our earthly scene were from the Sirius system, as both Sirians and our earth plane are well matched in terms of gravitational forces. Also with them now in close proximity to the earth are Pleiadians, Andromedans, Zetas, the Ashtar Command (the Federation's airborne division) and many others. Most members of the Galactic Federation are benevolent and are now here to assist Earth and those who choose to accompany her, in making their transition to a higher dimension with its attendant state of expanded consciousness.

The goals of the Galactic Federation are listed as follows:

1. To work with us in solving the problems of a threatened society due to an unbalanced state of technology that has not been unified with spirituality.

2. To encourage friendship with other advanced civilizations from other planets and dimensional realms visiting Earth in UFOs.

3. To assist us to repair the damage we have done to Earth's biosphere through our destructive pollution, our abuse of non-sustainable resources and our misuse of nuclear energy for military and other purposes.

4. To aid us in ending war, crime, poverty and disease.

It's important to note that the Galactic Federation will only offer its assistance in solving our problems. We must take the major part of the initiative ourselves, as these difficulties are entirely of our own making.

Again and again we hear the following, "If extraterrestrials are here to help us, why don't they show themselves openly and land in full view of the general public?" Would you come if you knew that the majority of the populace would be traumatized by fear, or that the military forces in a country you wish to assist would subject you to an immediate attack? Despite their technology, which is thousands of years in advance of ours, and their capability of avoiding an attack, The Galactic Federation's missions are peaceful. Our first contact will only be attempted by them when the majority of Earth's population is ready and our governments are themselves committed to peace.

It is a well documented fact that since the 1950s our major world governments have met with members of the Galactic Federation, whose suggestions for creating a peaceful world that is free from hunger, war and poverty have fallen on deaf ears. In addition, there has been a massive cover-up orchestrated by our governments, the media, religions, multi-nationals and the banking cartels, to enable these organizations to continue their exercise of power and control over the people and their ongoing manipulation of the global economic system.

When the Galactic Federation makes its first open contact with the people of Earth (and they will come when they judge the time to be right), greet them not in fear, but in joy and brotherhood. They are not conquering invaders, as Hollywood is so fond of portraying them. In these end times they come in peace, love and in service to our Divine Creator, for our greater benefit.

Mary Mageau has been actively walking the spiritual path for many years and has written articles for many on-line and off-line magazines and newsletters, including her own. She has extensive knowledge and she has shared a lot of valuable information in her excellent e-book, *Preparing For Ascension*, which she is generously making available free of charge. The link for obtaining her e-book is as follows: *http://www.thecominggoldenage. com/Preparing_For_Ascension.htm.* You may e-mail Mary at *km3highnote@bigpond.com.*

Chapter 24

Astral Travel

When I was a youth of age 14, I found myself going spontaneously out of the body. I was like a mind and a pair of eyes on the ceiling. I could travel and go on adventures.

I liked doing it until one morning, when I woke up paralyzed. I couldn't move a muscle. I was scared. That experience ended my out-of-body explorations. I shifted my interest to high school sports, social activities and studies.

Years later, when I read Journeys Out of the Body *and other related books, I learned there is a remedy when paralysis occurs. You allow yourself to go back to sleep and usually you will wake up back in your body and return to normal. Don't struggle.*

Naturally, I read Ann Miller's long interview with Anna in The Star Beacon *(April 2012) ("Astral explorer traverses space and time") with keen interest. Anna describes beings in other dimensions and worlds, including contact with UFOs. Fascinating. The following is Anna's story, used with her permission.*

EDITOR'S NOTE: Anna, who prefers that we not use her last name, travels out of body and through time. The following is what she shared with us in an interview about astral travel.

ANNA: My first out-of-body experience was about 15 years ago and I knew nothing about what an OBE was. I went from a dream state to full conscious awareness. At this moment I experienced traveling through a tunnel of magnificent colors. At the end of the tunnel I ended up in another world. It seemed like I was in a fairytale. The colors were brilliant. The sky had apricot/pinkish hues to it. Flowers, trees and foliage were everywhere. Also visible were several cottages. It was the most beautiful place I had ever seen.

I knew I was being guided by my higher self and I just walked into a cottage, which seemed very familiar to me. There was an entity-being lying on a table and I started doing hands-on energy work. At that time I did not know what hands-on energy work was. I was intrigued by that whole experience. It probably took me five years before I started asking questions ... to the Universe, such as "What was that?"

It turned out there was an OBE teacher named William Buhlman in Denver, who was providing a weekend seminar. I learned techniques from him and also from another experienced teacher in Fort Collins. I began practicing, and in about 30 days I had my first one.

TSB: Does it happen at night, during the day, or do you set up a time to intentionally ... ?

ANNA: I've found that the best time to do it is after you've had four to five hours of sleep. I practice my techniques usually from 3:00 to 7:00 A.M. I continued with the techniques every day for years. I've had hundreds of experiences and knew in the beginning of my travels I never wanted to stop doing this.

TSB: Were you afraid the first time it happened?

ANNA: No, I wasn't, because I had that "first" one.

TSB: And did it happen when you awoke? What were the circumstances for the very first one?

ANNA: My higher self woke me up in a dream state. It was at that moment I realized I had the same conscious awareness as I do in my waking hours in this incarnation. I got to experience and remember many details in that reality as I do my current 3D reality.

I've learned various techniques to help me explore many worlds. These meditation techniques helped me with focusing, building prana and raising my frequency.

You discover that your state of mind and emotions play a huge role in what type of environment and experience you will have. Typically what frequency you are vibrating at matches the reality you will be exploring.

TSB: You certainly don't want to be in some low frequency and run into some bad influences.

ANNA: It is possible, and with my experiences I've run into situations that are fearful at the time. But know you are protected. I almost always ask for angelic presence whenever I travel. I also have learned how powerful we are, and I visualize a shield of white light surrounding my body and carry with me the knowingness that I can confront any situation I am in with calmness and love and be safe in doing so.

Once you learn to separate your lighter energy body from your physical body, you can instantly be in a new environment. So, if you are in an environment that displeases you, you can leave that one and move on to another dimension or return to your physical body.

Most of the time it is a pleasant surprise in the reality you are experiencing. You will instantly know how to communicate telepathically. The difficulty comes when you want to retain all the details of your conversations.

When you travel, you will be meeting many beings from different worlds. Not all of them are human looking. Many times they may be in your bedroom—standing or sitting next to you. They are as curious about you as you are about them. Some of these beings know you and you will feel as though you know them also. I've experienced connections that have been powerful.

My OBE teacher told me that exploring other dimensions is similar to jumping into an ocean and seeing various kinds of fish. You are going to see many kinds of entities. And if that thought scares you, then don't bother trying it.

TSB: Are they in the physical then when they appear? To the point where someone else could see them?

ANNA: Yes, they may be vibrating at the same frequency as you. Higher frequency beings have the ability to lower their frequency to match yours. I have seen beings with my physical eyes. I had a being once whose frequency was so high, his light body was flashing in and out. I could only see the outer shell—not the eyes or nose. I could feel his presence. It was such a magnetic pull—so incredibly strong. Because his frequency was so high, I wasn't vibrating at the same frequency as he was.

TSB: I want to ask about the silver cord. I've read that we all have a silver cord when we astral travel (that connects us to our physical body).

ANNA: I have seen it on an animal once, but on myself ... to turn around and look ... I've never really looked for it. I'm not focused on it.

TSB: What do you think it is?

ANNA: I believe the silver cord is a light cord connecting our physical body to our lighter energy bodies. We have multidimensional bodies. We can access our various energy bodies by intention and asking.

TSB: What I'm curious about is, are you aware of a body when you're traveling?

ANNA: Sometimes you do travel with a body and sometimes you are pure consciousness, with just a light body. At times I've looked at my body and I've seen something very similar to my physical body. And then there's other times when you may want to experience a past life—another lifetime—and you will have totally different clothes, opposite gender, etc. There are times when, if I'm looking at my hands, I just see shimmering sparkles of light.

TSB: Would you describe that as your etheric body or light body?

ANNA: I would consider that as the higher self ... the soul.

TSB: You've traveled to other planets, I assume. And does that happen in just the blink of an eye? It doesn't take much time at all, does it?

ANNA: No, because we have omnipresence. We can be anywhere we choose to be instantaneous ... with just a thought.

For the first few years, my higher self and my guides chose where I needed to go. Now I'm more specific in what I want to do with it because I've spent so much time exploring and seeing things that are just not of this world.

I'm more focused on being here on Earth and helping with the transition. It's different now ... I don't practice on a daily basis like I did for years and years ... but I do practice periodically.

TSB: So do you sort of go in stages, like you might go several months without practicing it and then get back into it?

ANNA: If you really want to learn how to do this and have a lot of experiences, I recommend you practice every day, for at least half an hour. After a while it's much easier to bring one on.

TSB: Probably the first thing you have to learn is meditation and how to quiet your mind.

ANNA: How to quiet your mind ... and how to focus. Focusing is very, very important once you're out of body, because your thoughts control how you move, how you act. One thing that happens with a lot of travelers is as soon as you think of your physical body, you're immediately right back into your body.

TSB: So that would take a lot of discipline, I think.

ANNA: It does. You need to set the intention and

block out all distractions. That's why I think early in the morning is best, when your house is quiet and the phone is not going off. You absolutely have to do away with the fear. The fear is a big blockage for anyone wanting to do this.

TSB: How long does it take a normal trip?

ANNA: A "normal" trip? You can be fully conscious in a situation for maybe five seconds, or there are other times when it seems like you've been out for hours.

I know there are times when I've been exploring cities and other worlds and it feels like I've been gone for a whole day. Time ... you can't really describe it once you're there.

I know that in my own experiences, there were many situations I would have given anything just to be able to stay out longer so that I could gather more information and experience what I saw, what I felt and who I was with.

TSB: Is there a difference between when you astral travel the way you do, and what we do in our sleep? Do you think everybody does this?

ANNA: I do. I think it does happen often with everyone.

TSB: But most the time we don't remember ...

ANNA: We don't remember. And there are certain people who come back with little tidbits of information. Once you learn how to do this, you can set the intention to remember all the details.

TSB: In Suzy Ward's books, Matthew talks about Nirvana and how we go there at night for visits, but we don't remember.

ANNA: Most of us don't. But once you practice this and become very good at it, you will remember more of your visits. I've met almost all of my deceased relatives and I even met friends from high school … some of them I didn't really know in school, but when you're out there you just think of them and instantly you are right next to them. I met a deceased classmate who was thinking, "What the heck are you doing here?"

TSB: Can you describe what it's like there? It's pretty nice, I hear.

ANNA: Oh, it's just magnificent.

TSB: It's just another world, really.

ANNA: It is, it's actually right here. The colors are more vibrant, very peaceful … it's Paradise. I can't wait to go back and visit more and more. There have been a few times … when I have actually become aware, in a room with many people … I recognize a lot of them, not only from this lifetime but from other lifetimes. We are together in soul gatherings. Most likely they're not aware that their soul was having this experience.

TSB: But the soul remembers.

ANNA: Exactly, the soul remembers.

TSB: Do you ever feel like you want to go there and

stay? That you don't want to return to your body? Is there a temptation factor there?

ANNA: A few times, yes, especially when you find a loved one that you have a deep connection with.

TSB: Such as your twin? Met him (or her)?

ANNA: I'm under the belief that we have more than one soulmate. Connecting with a soulmate is an intense blending of energies. It's a very precious moment. You never forget these.

TSB: Do you think that what is going to happen, possibly at the end of this year, as we move into a higher experience and focus, do you think more and more people are going to be able to do what you do, without a whole lot of effort?

ANNA: Yes, it's going to be a re-remembering, to know how to do this.

TSB: Have you been in the future?

ANNA: Yes, I have. This happened before I even knew about a transition. This was probably about seven years ago, when I wanted to explore this possibility. I set the intention to go into the future, and the next thing I know, I am in an intense electrical storm where I can see electrical currents going everywhere. I can hear crackling noises. I went right back into my physical body because I wasn't expecting that.
The next day I said, "I'm going to do this." I went a couple hundred years into the future. I was a man

... and I was standing right in front of my wife and my sister and her husband. We were doing research in what is considered Australia now, and they were explaining everything that was going on. I was just totally amazed by the whole experience. I looked right at them, eye to eye, and I said, "How can this be? How does this work? Please help me understand this." And they were telling me that I am similar to what a doctor would do, studying white blood cells and red blood cells, and they told me I was also connected to a Vega starship and planet. At that time I had never even heard of Vega. I was just floored by the whole experience.

TSB: Do you document your experiences?

ANNA: I stopped documenting my experiences about five years ago. I was having so many that it just wasn't necessary any more. My experiences are now within me. It's an amazing universe. Everybody can do this. Our typical life is pretty mundane compared to what we have to wake up to.

TSB: Is there any kind of danger for people who are interested in this, who want to try it and don't have any training?

ANNA: The only thing I would recommend is if somebody is going through a lot of emotional trauma and their frequency is very low, you're going to attract low frequency beings, and they're definitely there. And you may see them and feel them. It won't be a pleasant experience. You're not going to be harmed, but it won't be the highlight of your travels.

I always got into the habit of raising my frequency,

such as turning on music that moves me, or I may focus on a memory ... a person or an animal. I would do something to get my mind set into a calm and peaceful state ... connection to the Creator ... to God.

ANNA: Before I even learned about extraterrestrials—star brothers and sisters—I became fully aware on many ships. And they were wonderful experiences. I was told I was Pleiadian, even before I knew what that was. I have connections to other beings too, and I've met other beings from other worlds ... many of us have also. They're here to learn through us.

TSB: Why do you think the space brothers and sisters care about us? Why are they here?

ANNA: Because we're all part of one big family. When we leave this planet, there are going to be many of us who are going to help out on other worlds.

TSB: So there are other planets throughout the galaxy and beyond that have been in the state that Earth is now, going through its difficulty, and they've been there to help those.

ANNA: Yes, I have been told this is so. We are star beings too.

TSB: Do you believe there are renegade beings or some that are not so helpful that would exploit us, and how are we protected?

ANNA: Yes, there are renegade beings. We are protected by our galactic brothers and sisters. They are assisting us with our transition to the new Earth.

TSB: People talk about alien invasions, and you see so many of those kinds of movies, and I think that if they had meant to take us over, it would have happened long ago.

ANNA: Sure, and there are some that would have loved to. The opportunity for a takeover no longer exists.

TSB: So we are all a part of this whole cosmic picture and that is why they care.

ANNA: We are all connected to each other. We help one another out during difficult times. It's the spiritual thing to do!

If you wish to subscribe to *The Star Beacon*, Ann Ulrich Miller's bimonthly publication on UFOs and all things metaphysical, visit Earth Star Publication's Web site at *www.earthstarpublications.com*. A year's subscription to the print version is $27 (US), $30 (Canada) or $36 (foreign), but you can also get the full-color PDF version anywhere in the world for just $12. Email Ann at *starbeacon@gmail.com*.

Appendix

9 JUL 47

DIRECTIVE TO LIEUTENANT GENERAL TWINING

You will proceed to the White Sands Proving Ground Command Center without delay for the purpose of making an appraisal of the reported unidentified objects being kept there. Part of your mission there will deal with the military, political and psychological situations -current and projected. In the course of your survey you will maintain liaison with the military officials in the area.

In making your appraisal it is desired that you proceed with detachment from any opinions or feelings expressed by personnel involved which do not conform to sound reasoning with regard to the possible outcome. In presenting the findings of your mission you should endeavor to state as concisely as possible your estimate of the character, extent, and probable consequences in the event that assistance is not given.

When your mission in New Mexico is completed you will proceed on a brief trip to the Sandia AEC facility to make an appraisal of the situation there, also of the reaction by the Los Alamos people involved. Before going to White Sands you will communicate with General Eisenhower to ascertain whether he desires you to proceed via Kirtland AAF.

You will take with you such experts, technicians, scientists and assistants as you deem necessary to the effectiveness of your mission.

Approved
Harry Truman

July 9, 1947

Directive to Lieutenant General Twining, July 9, 1947

TOP SECRET
EYES ONLY.

THE WHITE HOUSE
WASHINGTON

September 24, 1947.

MEMORANDUM FOR THE SECRETARY OF DEFENSE

Dear Secretary Forrestal:

As per our recent conversation on this matter, you are hereby authorized to proceed with all due speed and caution upon your undertaking. Hereafter this matter shall be referred to only as Operation Majestic Twelve.

It continues to be my feeling that any future considerations relative to the ultimate disposition of this matter should rest solely with the Office of the President following appropriate discussions with yourself, Dr. Bush and the Director of Central Intelligence.

[signature: Harry Truman]

TOP SECRET
EYES ONLY

00 883

Memorandum for the Secretary of Defense
September 24, 1947

TOP SECRET / MAJIC
EYES ONLY
• TOP SECRET •

COPY ONE OF ONE.

SUBJECT: OPERATION MAJESTIC-12 PRELIMINARY BRIEFING FOR PRESIDENT-ELECT EISENHOWER.

DOCUMENT PREPARED 18 NOVEMBER, 1952.

BRIEFING OFFICER: ADM. ROSCOE H. HILLENKOETTER (MJ-1)

NOTE: This document has been prepared as a preliminary briefing only. It should be regarded as introductory to a full operations briefing intended to follow.

• • • • • •

OPERATION MAJESTIC-12 is a TOP SECRET Research and Development/ Intelligence operation responsible directly and only to the President of the United States. Operations of the project are carried out under control of the Majestic-12 (Majic-12) Group which was established by special classified executive order of President Truman on 24 September, 1947, upon recommendation by Dr. Vannevar Bush and Secretary James Forrestal. (See Attachment "A".) Members of the Majestic-12 Group were designated as follows

Adm. Roscoe H. Hillenkoetter
Dr. Vannevar Bush
Secy. James V. Forrestal*
Gen. Nathan F. Twining
Gen. Hoyt S. Vandenberg
Dr. Detlev Bronk
Dr. Jerome Hunsaker
Mr. Sidney W. Souers
Mr. Gordon Gray
Dr. Donald Menzel
Gen. Robert M. Montague
Dr. Lloyd V. Berkner

The death of Secretary Forrestal on 22 May, 1949, created a vacancy which remained unfilled until 01 August, 1950, upon which date Gen. Walter B. Smith was designated as permanent replacement.

• TOP SECRET •
TOP SECRET / MAJIC
EYES ONLY

T52-EXEMPT (E)

Operation Majestic 12, briefing for President-Elect Eisenhower

The Majestic Documents (Evidence That We Are Not Alone)

Introduction to the Majestic Documents

by **Ryan and Robert Wood**

MajesticDocuments.com is a groundbreaking look at the United States UFO program called Majestic and the top secret government documents that tell the story of presidential and military action, authorization, and cover-up regarding UFOs and their alien occupants. A remarkable work of investigative journalism, this Web site is the first to authenticate top secret UFO documents that tell a detailed story of the crashed discs, alien bodies, presidential briefings, and superb secrecy. Special attention is paid to the forensic authentication issues of content, provenance, type, style and chronology. The story the documents tell leaves the reader with little doubt that the cover-up is real, shocking, and at times unethical.

Operation Majestic-12 was established by special classified presidential order on September 24, 1947 at the recommendation of Secretary of Defense James Forrestal and Dr. Vannevar Bush, Chairman of the Joint Research and Development Board. The goal of the group was to exploit everything they could from recovered alien technology.

Buried in a super-secret "MAJIC EYES ONLY" classification that was above TOP SECRET—long before the modern top secret code word special access programs of today—Major General Leslie R. Groves (who commanded the Manhattan Project to deliver the atomic bomb) kept just one copy of the details of crashed alien technology in his safe in Washington, D.C.

Ambitious, elite scientists such as Vannevar Bush, Albert Einstein, and Robert Oppenheimer, and career military people such as Hoyt Vandenberg, Roscoe Hillenkoetter, Leslie Groves, and George Marshall, along with a select cast of other experts, feverishly and secretively labored to understand the alien agenda, technology, and their implications.

Einstein and Oppenheimer were called in to give their opinion, drafting a six-page paper titled "Relationships With Inhabitants Of Celestial Bodies." They provided prophetic insight into our modern nuclear strategies and satellites, and expressed agitated urgency that an agreement be reached with the President so that scientists could proceed to study the alien technology.

The extraordinary recovery of fallen airborne objects in the state of New Mexico, between July 4 and July 6, 1947, caused the Chief of Staff of the Army Air Force's Interplanetary Phenomena Unit, Scientific and Technical Branch, Counterintelligence Directorate to initiate a thorough investigation. The special unit was formed in 1942 in response to two crashes in the Los Angeles area in late February 1942. The draft summary report begins, "At 2332 MST, 3 July 47, radar stations in east Texas and White Sands Proving Ground, N.M. tracked two unidentified aircraft until they both dropped off radar. Two crash sites have been located close to the WSPG. Site LZ-1 was located at a ranch near Corona, Approx. 75 miles northwest of the town of Roswell. Site LZ-2 was located approx. 20 miles southeast of the town of Socorro, at latitude 33-40-31 and longitude 106-28-29."

The first-ever-known UFO crash retrieval case occurred in 1941 in Cape Girardeau, Missouri. This crash kicked off early reverse-engineering work, but it did not create a unified intelligence effort to exploit possible technological gains apart from the Manhattan Project uses.

The debris from the primary field of the 1947 crash 20 miles southeast of Socorro, New Mexico was called ULAT-1 (Unidentified Lenticular Aerodyne Technology), and it excited metallurgists with its unheard-of tensile and sheer strengths. The fusion nuclear (called neutronic at that time) engine used heavy water and deuterium with an oddly arranged series of coils, magnets, and electrodes—descriptions that resemble the "cold fusion" studies of today.

Harry Truman kept the technical briefing documents of September 24, 1947 for further study, pondering the challenges of creating and funding a secret organization before the CIA existed (although the Central Intelligence Group or CIG did exist) and before there was a legal procedure of funding non-war operations.

In April 1954, a group of senior officers of the U.S. intelligence community and the Armed Forces gathered for one of the most secret and sensational briefings in history. The subject was Unidentified Flying Objects—not just a discussion of sightings, but how to recover crashed UFOs, where to ship the parts, and how to deal with the occupants. For example, in the "Special Operations Manual (SOM1-01) Extraterrestrial Entities Technology Recovery and Disposal," MAJESTIC-12 "red teams" mapped out UFO crash retrieval scenarios with special attention given to press blackouts, body packaging, and live alien transport, isolation, and custody.

MajesticDocuments.com is not another rehash of the famous Roswell story—it contains over 500 pages (and growing) of newly surfaced documents, many of which date years before the Roswell crash. Unlike other Web sites, a central theme of validating authenticity is woven throughout the site while telling the exciting story of the U.S. government's work on retrieval and analysis of extraterrestrial hardware and alien life forms from 1941 to present.

Our Compact Disc (CD), *The Secret: Evidence That We Are Not Alone,* shows 117 pages of "leaked" top secret UFO documents, most of them never before seen by the public. Some 26 pages were allegedly prepared for a 1954 Special Operations Manual (SOM1-01). This can be purchased on our Web site along with two other books that provide both the raw original documents and retyped replicas that are often easier to read. The CD provides an initial discussion as to why this briefing manual and the other documents are almost certainly authentic.

The Majestic documents tell a mind-boggling story of deception, intelligence and counterintelligence, revolutionary alien technology, missing nuclear weapons, and compartmentalized secrecy spanning in time from the first crashed disc retrieval in 1941 until three days before President Kennedy's assassination in 1963.

Our investigation team, led by Robert and Ryan Wood—a father and son team with 50 years of combined UFO study—has applied their skills as both sleuths and scholars. Painstakingly verifying "deep throat" sources, meticulously analyzing old and controversial documents, they arrive finally at conclusions that are as well grounded in fact as they are stunning in their implications.

UFO-related secret programs have consumed a significant part of America's black budget since the Manhattan Project. The 1997 government-disclosed intelligence budget portion alone is $26 billion and according to Tim Weiner's 1990 book *Blank Check*, the total black-budget was about $35 billion in 1990. Even the most sensational conspiracy of modern times—the Kennedy assassination—is likely linked to the UFO cover-up and the military cabal, as several of the documents demonstrate.

Overall, the United States UFO program grew out of necessity. First, to determine the alien threat, second to exploit their advanced technology in any way we could to gain a military, economic or even a psychological advantage and win World War II, and third to maintain power, authority, and control of both technology, governments, and world stability. Initially, to make the project public would have sent unpredictable turmoil into science, religion, politics, and global economics.

Even the most hardened skeptic, after reviewing the data presented and seeing copies of the original documents, will find it hard to deny the reality of military and government cover-up for over 50 years. All of the usual questions, which the thoughtful skeptical reader has, have either already been addressed or soon will be in our ongoing research. We welcome Web site visitors—comments, criticism, and support.

Source:
http://www.majesticdocuments.com/documents/intro.php

Citizens Against UFO Secrecy

Peter A. Gersten, Esq.
Attorney for Plaintiff
Arizona Bar #016925
Sedona, Arizona 86351

UNITED STATES DISTRICT COURT
THE DISTRICT OF ARIZONA

CITIZENS AGAINST UFO SECRECY, INC.	)	
7349 Via Paseo Del Sur #515-194	)	
Scottsdale, Arizona 85258	)	
(602) 818-8248	)	CIV98-0538PHXROS
	)	
Plaintiff,	)	
	)	AFFIDAVIT
v.	)	
	)	
	)	
	)	
DEPARTMENT OF ARMY	)	
	)	
Defendant,	)	

I, Col. Philip J. Corso, (Ret.) do hereby swear, under the penalties of perjury, that the following statements are true:

That at all times hereinafter mentioned, I was a member and officer of the defendant.

That during my tenure with the defendant I was a member of President Eisenhower's National Security Council and former head of the Foreign Technology Desk at defendant's Research & Development department.

That on or about July 6, 1947, while stationed at Fort Riley, Kansas, I personally observed a four-foot non-human creature with bizarre-looking four-fingered hands, thin legs and feet, and an oversized incandescent light bulb-shaped head. The eye sockets were oversized and almond shaped and pointed down to its tiny nose. The creature's skull was overgrown to the point where all its facial features were arranged frontally, occupying only a small circle on the lower part of the head. There were no eyebrows or any indications of facial hair. The creature had only a tiny flat slit for a mouth and it was

http://www.caus.org/FOIA/CorsoAffidavit.htm

165

completely closed, resembling more of a crease or indentation between the nose and the bottom of the chinless skull than a fully functioning orifice.

That in 1961, I came into possession of what I refer to as the 'Roswell File.' This file contained field reports, medical autopsy reports and technological debris from the crash an extraterrestrial vehicle in Roswell, New Mexico in 1947.

That I have personally read the medical autopsy reports which refer to the autopsy of the previously described creature that I saw in 1947 at Fort Riley, Kansas.

That said autopsy reports indicated the autopsy was performed at Walter Reed Hospital, which was under the authority of the defendant at the time of the autopsy.

That said autopsy report referred to the creature as an 'extraterrestrial biological entity.'

_____

Colonel Philip J. Corso (ret.)

Sworn before me
this day of ___ May, 1998.

_____

Image of the actual page with Coro's signature and Notary seal

Return to CAUS.ORG

Col. Philip J. Corso Dead at age 83

Update — July 17, 1998

CAUS thanks CNI News and Michael Lindemann for this update:

Col. Philip J. Corso (U.S. Army, ret.) died of a heart attack at approximately 11:15 pm EDT on Thursday, July 16, 1998. He was 83.

Corso, who was widely known for his controversial 1997 book, *The Day After Roswell*, suffered a massive heart attack in early June of this year but made a remarkable recovery.

He was at home on Tuesday, July 15 and was said to be feeling fine when he apparently suffered a second heart attack at about 9:00 am. He was taken to a hospital in nearby Palm Beach, Florida for treatment, but his condition deteriorated. Doctors decided to transfer him on Thursday evening to Jupiter Medical Center, where he had been treated for his earlier attack. Col. Corso reportedly died at about the time he reached the Jupiter facility.

"He really wanted to stay," Corso's son, Philip Jr., told CNI News in a phone call on Friday afternoon. "The last three weeks (since the first attack) have been very productive. I knew he had more to say, and he told me a great deal" about the Roswell UFO incident, Philip Jr. said.

Unpublished manuscripts and other UFO-related information left by Col. Corso will be protected and made available in due course to researchers and the public, Philip Jr. said. "This is what my father lived for," he added.

Colonel Corso, a highly decorated soldier, will be buried in a military cemetery near Orlando, Florida. He is survived by two children, four grandchildren and one great-grandchild.

Aztec, New Mexico Crash Site

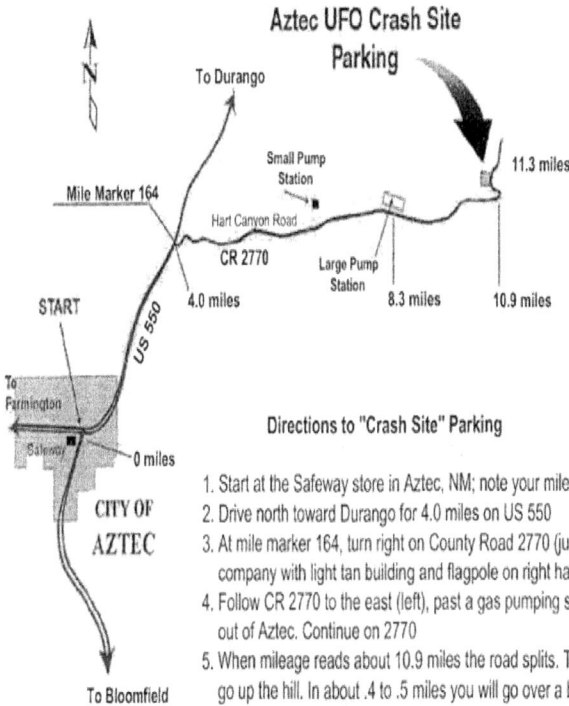

Aztec UFO Crash Site Parking

To Durango

Small Pump Station

11.3 miles

Mile Marker 164

Hart Canyon Road

CR 2770

Large Pump Station

START

4.0 miles

8.3 miles

10.9 miles

To Farmington

Safeway

0 miles

CITY OF AZTEC

To Bloomfield

Directions to "Crash Site" Parking

1. Start at the Safeway store in Aztec, NM; note your mileage
2. Drive north toward Durango for 4.0 miles on US 550
3. At mile marker 164, turn right on County Road 2770 (just past construction company with light tan building and flagpole on right hand side of highway)
4. Follow CR 2770 to the east (left), past a gas pumping station about 8.3 miles out of Aztec. Continue on 2770
5. When mileage reads about 10.9 miles the road splits. Take the left fork and go up the hill. In about .4 to .5 miles you will go over a bumpy cattle guard. Just after that is a parking lot on the left. Pull into it. You are facing west.
6. From here it is about 1/3 mile walk. Get out of the car and walk south. Start down a small path that will go west and connect with a small dirt road in a few hundred feet. Continue on the dirt road west till you come to a barbed wire fence (200-300yards). Going left along the fence you will come to a gate; go through it and close it. You are now on a bike trail. Follow it to the left. In a short distance, on the right you will see a metal plaque on a stand set in concrete that commemorates what may have happened on this site.

169

James Parsons
James Parsons Fine Arts
PO Box 1272
El Prado, NM 87529-1272
(575) 751-0073

Working on the DEW Line

Nov. 26, 2004

Jim interviewed Herb Mott, an old-time illustrator, now retired. Mott did 65 commissions for the US Air Force, he told Jim, some of these hanging in the Pentagon and at Air Force bases around the country. "I can't just illustrate anything," Mott said; "I have to like the assignment to do a good job." In 1956 the Air Force flew Mott to Thule in Greenland to complete a commission for the Air Force collection. Mott was taken to Thule in the C-124, Jim's old aircraft. Jim flew 12 missions as crew navigator to secret bases in the arctic in 1955. Jim commissioned Mott to paint "Working on the Dew Line" for Jim's personal collection. Almost all Veterans are proud of their military service to the country and Jim is no exception. "It was exciting and dangerous work," Jim said, about those long strenuous days—"an experience I'll never forget."

Desiderata

by Billy

NOTE: In today's times, which are rife with emotion and yet emotionally cold, we offer you these unique passages (Desiderata = desirable and vital items) of beautiful and poignant words by "Billy" Eduard Albert Meier, and wish you all that is expressed herein.

Included with our sincere wishes is a request that you photocopy these words of Billy as often as possible and as you deem appropriate. Please mail the text to your family members, relatives, friends, colleagues, acquaintances—simply to everyone whose address you may have.

With our friendly greetings and sincerest best wishes for the remainder of your life,

FIGU (Semjase-Silver-Star-Center, Hinterschmidruti, CH-8495 Schmidruti email: info@figu.ch

Pay heed to freedom, for it is the privilege and prerogative of every human being and all other life forms. Pay heed to love, for it is the essence of Creation, of human beings and of life. Pay heed to peace, for it is the assurance of all positive development and unrestricted evolution. Pay heed to harmony, for therein lies the equilibrium of every thought, feeling, deed and everything else.

Do not allow yourself to be rushed by the din, burdens or bustle of daily living, but remain always composed under every circumstance life presents. Seek tranquility, peace, love and freedom—each is a valuable element of harmony. Allot some time every day to finding tranquility, for it affords you respite and time to contemplate.

Practice getting along well with everyone, but do not lose yourself in the process, and always remain within the limits of your ability. Always respect your fellowmen as fellow human beings, although they may have dispositions that differ from yours; indeed, even the worst among them is a creation of Creation, hence, everyone is just like you—a human being. State your truths freely, clearly, calmly and candidly, for only in this manner is an authentic picture created which defines the true nature of everything.

Allow other people to freely express their opinions, for they are allotted the same rights as you. Listen to others, to the bright and intellectual individuals, and also to the obtuse, the foolish and those who lack learning, for they, too, have opinions and statements to offer. But distance yourself from aggressive, boisterous and obstinate individuals so as not to become embroiled in their pointless disputes, for such people insult one's consciousness, humaneness and refinement; and yet, at the same time, forget not that they too are beings of Creation, whom you, as a fellow human being, must show appropriate respect, even though you may find their thoughts, feelings, deeds and actions unacceptable. Should you draw comparisons between yourself and others, you will inevitably realize that others are either stronger or weaker than you in certain matters; this, however, is no justification for you to feel superior or inferior to them. Therefore, neither vain nor arrogant become, neither bitter nor ashamed, for there will always be someone who is more eminent or less advanced than you in learning, morality, character and the like.

Refrain not from enjoying achievements you have gained through your own honest efforts. Delight in these accomplishments as much as you do in setting positive objectives and bringing them to successful completions. Always be mindful of continuing your development in every possible matter, including both your personal and consciousness-related evolutions. Therefore he perpetually and humbly attentive to your personal progress, but only in a righteous manner, because integrity is the only, truly positive possession you have as a human being in these changing times.

Approach your work and your business with forethought and circumspection, for good work is worthy of proper compensation; circumspection, forethought and honesty offer sound long-term rewards in business, even in a world of guile. When you achieve positive, remarkable successes, keep from becoming blinded and deafened by them and proceed toward those things of virtuous substance. Be attentive also to the means and ways of the people with whom you deal; though many strive for lofty ideals, few reach their goals. Life appears filled with heroism wherever you gaze, but when you glance behind the scenes, you find only fear enveloped in a haze and someone's craving for pretending to be greater than he or she really is. Hence, heed not these matters to the degree where you wish to imitate them; instead, recognize your true self. Positively realize yourself within your own Self. And allow these traits to permeate your entire nature. Do not feign affection for someone if, in reality, you fail to hold such feelings for the person. Make no pretense to your fellowmen that bears no truth, for honesty is a directive which, together with knowledge, is undeniably the path to wisdom.

Never be cynical about sincere love, for love provides

you with the certainty of co-existing within everything there is, in both the spiritual and the physical realms. And love is the true essence of Creation; it will endure for *ur-eternity* and all Great Times beyond every conceivable hardship and disappointment. Love is the actual cornerstone and the true incentive of life where the aspirations form to reach higher, indeed, to the very highest levels possible. Love will never die, it will survive eternally as it pulsates in the everlasting rhythm of Creational harmony.

Forfeit every negative trait in your life with dignity and, through self-knowledge, leave yourself open to counsel for self-realization. Cheerfully accept what your positive knowledge and balanced wisdom counsel you to do, and gain control over your thoughts, feelings, indeed, your entire consciousness, for in so doing you strengthen yourself for unavoidable predicaments, and you will never lose heart even when faced with unexpected misfortune.

Always practice loyalty and integrity, and never make yourself unhappy over unrighteous things or those you merely imagine. Free yourself from alarm and fear, which oftentimes originate from loneliness, mental exhaustion and idleness. Loneliness, mental exhaustion and idleness are enemies of progress. Seek, therefore, the company of those who are knowledgeable and wise, for they will teach you how to stimulate and utilize your thoughts, and how to actively evolve.

Always practice healthy self-discipline while being kind to yourself at all times, for you are an individual, an independent person, who requires not only the pleasant kindness of others but also the consideration you provide yourself. You are a creation of Creation, the universe, and in no way are you any less than your fellowman, the trees, plants, all animal species or the celestial bodies in the infinite vastness of universal space.

You have the right to be alive and to exist on this Earth, regardless of who and what you may be, and it matters not if you comprehend the unfolding of the universe in the way Creation, the Universal Consciousness, intends it. Nothing unfolds without Creation's love, and it will not do so unless it is within the framework of the Creation-given laws and directives. Accept, then, that you only exist because this is how it was intended to be and because predetermined for you through the *ur-eternally* everlasting, Creational plan.

Live, therefore, in freedom, love, peace and harmony among similar-minded individuals and with all of Creation's creatures. Live also in peace, love, freedom and harmony with Creation, regardless of what you may perceive Creation to be. Live also in peace, love, freedom, and harmony with yourself, your psyche and your personality—regardless of your deeds, thoughts, feelings, contemplations and aspirations throughout the rigors of daily life. Never lose sight of this, regardless of all the hurriedness, drudgery, disappointment, broken dreams, negations and tears. In spite of the turmoil surrounding you, the world is indeed beautiful and life is worth living.

About the Author

James A. Parsons was a Celestial navigator in the United States Air Force and a technical writer, who also worked in the aerospace industry. He graduated from the University of New Mexico and received a law degree from the University of Denver.

James became a full-time art dealer in Denver in 1964, a gallery owner and an art appraiser. His aesthetic awareness, integrity and business skills connected him to art lovers around the world and made him an inspiring, generous and exacting mentor to a new generation of art dealers.

James came to Taos in the 1970s. *The Art Fever* is his first book, capturing the pleasure and the excitement of the art world and those who make it their life.

An adventurous and compassionate man, a traveler and a seeker of truth, James was fascinated with metaphysical studies, especially the teachings of Edgar Cayce.

Sadly, he left this world on May 5, 2013, shortly before this book was published. He will be greatly missed.

Ursula Freer, Cover Artist

Ursula Freer's lifelong involvement as a painter influences her digital art, giving her work a painterly quality.

She enjoys experimenting with a myriad of techniques to keep her work and interest fresh. Sometimes she uses translucent layered images to express the complexity of the subject matter.

As an environmentalist, the natural world is her favorite subject.

Consciousness and the sciences are also of great interest, thus ufology and the paranormal hold a special fascination for her.

While working with James on an art exhibit in Taos, New Mexico, Ursula was impressed with his extraordinary integrity and kindness. She feels so privileged to have her art on his book cover.

Ursula lives in Santa Fe, New Mexico, with her husband, a writer.

She has exhibited in the United States and internationally since 1986. Visit her art Web site at **http://ursulafreer.com**

Bella and Jim on their wedding day

Index

J-K

L-M

N-O

W